Hayes over New Zealand

New Edition

Hugh Hanafi Hayes

Hanafi Hayes

Hayes over New Zealand
Copyright © Hugh Hanafi Hayes

All Rights Reserved
Except for the purposes of fair reviewing, no part of this book may be reproduced in any form including, information storage or retrieval systems without permission in writing from the copyright owner and publisher of this book.

The author asserts his moral rights.

First published 1981
This edition published 2012

Original cover by John McNulty restored by Hamdani Milas

Also by the same author

Master Control
One Child's War
Mr Callaghan and the Asylum Seeker

VIII

Acknowledgements:

My thanks to my wife, Ardilah, for her patience and support. And to my colleague, Hamdani Milas for his technical and editorial advice in producing this book.

x

Preface

"They say I'm old fashioned and live in the past,
but sometimes I think progress progresses too fast."
Dr Seuss

ANY KIWI READERS OVER fifty will probably remember the wry but slightly derogatory quip that some used to put New Zealand down.

Airline captain to passengers: "We are starting our descent into New Zealand, please fasten your seat belts and put your watches back ten years".

I remember it, even though I arrived by sea and my first sight of New Zealand was spoilt a tad by the sad spectacle of the stricken inter-island ferry Wahine, lying half submerged where it had foundered on Barrett Reef in Wellington harbour.

Once disembarked from RMS Ruahine, which was also, ironically on its last journey as a passenger ship, I was immediately introduced to the New Zealand way of the 1960s.

I was travelling with my wife and five children of varying ages from six years down. We had everything we possessed with us either on our bodies or in big heavy sea chests.

In the customs shed, I learned a very important aspect of Kiwi culture. Do It Yourself. With a big strong-looking customs officer looking on, I was ordered, not requested, ordered, to heave each of our huge chests up onto the counter and unlock it for inspection. I even had to open the top for the man and once he had rifled through everything, searching for anything that might start an epidemic of foot and mouth disease, I had to close the top and heave it down onto the ground again. He offered no help at all. I got the distinct impression that he really didn't want anyone coming into his country if they looked like they were planning to stay.

But we got in and were met by friends, all driving old cars.

Remember the sixties and seventies? We all drove old bangers. Well nearly all of us. Real estate agents were a wee bit more upmarket.

However, this was the country that I learned to love, even though I never really accepted the common phrase of "She'll be right." Didn't take too kindly to the sandflies either. Nor the fact that teachers could still use corporal punishment to get their way, or a family holiday may well have meant a few days in a rented flea-ridden bach, where a cup of tea was made by putting an electrified poker in a pot of water 'til it boiled or blew up.

I had entered a society where most people painted their own homes, mended their own bangers, and travelled in the same domestic airplane cabin as the Prime Minister. A place with a charm all its own. One, to be honest, I didn't always appreciate at the time, like that initial period when I started my career in broadcasting as a radio announcer and newsreader - almost always asked to do the first shift. That meant for me and my dear wife, rising at around 4 am each morning in our simple house in NaeNae, or gnat gnat, in Lower Hutt.

You see I had to catch the first train, or unit as it was called, that got me to Wellington in time to either open up a radio station and play records or read the six a.m. news. The main reason I didn't fully appreciate it was that in order to get to the local station in time to catch that train, I had the prospect of running for twenty minutes with a bit of toast in my hand or, if I was lucky and he was passing, hitching a ride with the milkman. Sometimes all the effort was compounded by stress when the train was running late.

However, what I call Kiwi nous had to be learned and utilized. I recall how on one occasion, when I was due in to read the 6 a.m. news and the stopping train was running late, when the guard came and clicked my ticket, I told him my dilemma; I would be late and the nation would have its news delayed. Enough said. Without saying a word to me, the man disappeared through the door linking my carriage with the others and within seconds it seemed, the train picked up frightening speed, almost leaping off the rails and stopping for no one until it roared into Wellington Station giving me enough time to get to Broadcasting House and be sitting behind the microphone with a sheath of news in my hand waiting for the cue. Only in New Zealand could that happen to provide me with one of my fondest memories.

Now, though I can reflect on so many things that were unique to this country and its people, particularly when I moved from radio to television and was able to get out and about.

This was the time when as a features and documentary filmmaker I flourished, travelling all over the country, seeing places I fell in love with and meeting characters who fascinated, infuriated and inspired me. Much of which is recorded in *Hayes over New Zealand*.

My cameraman of that period, a young Aucklander Hamdani Milas, experienced almost the same sense of fulfillment and certainly the same love of place and people. The natural fusion of talents became the *raison d'être* for our establishing a small film company in Christchurch, where later we were joined by a certain Hammond Peek who learned his sound recording skills in that very simple environment.

Well now of course, New Zealand is no longer ten years behind the rest of the world. Its citizens drive the latest cars and allow mechanics to repair them. But call me old fashioned like Dr Seuss, I still remember with fondness most of the old bangers that I owned. I also treasured my iconic quarter-acre block, where I grew vegies and I backed to the hilt local government restrictions on the height of buildings. So I still have my nostalgic memory, even if that notion has been abandoned and the quarter acre has now been sub-divided or completely surrendered to high rise apartment blocks, high rise prices, for those who can afford them and high rise rentals and high rise unemployment for those who can't.

What of the local dairy? That natural meeting place for local gossip, tall tales and small sales. But what an array: newspapers, sweeties, bread, fireworks, cigarettes, mouse traps and even milk. Though there was no real pressure on anyone to buy anything if they had something to chat about from the neighbourhood. Will it, can it, survive the 'progress that progresses too fast' and dominates mainstream anywhere. Westfields shopping centres; the many coloured Warehouse sheds; Harvey Normans everything. Oh dear, I fear the 'personal' has been taken out of the shopping experience, although the personal cheque or credit card is still very welcome.

Back when it was ten years behind everywhere else, there were no McDonalds, just the humble meat pie or baked bean sandwich. So often I had been driving along some part of the West Coast for instance feeling a bit peckish, yearning for a meat pie, and on one occasion I particularly remember, suddenly spotting a sign that declared Hot Pies Here. With the saliva gathering in my mouth I had braked hard only to find another sign under the Hot Pies Here, saying: Closed. Kiwi humour.

That was the charm that couldn't be ignored and probably why most kiwis of that period were lean and healthy. Not like today I hear. Apparently health authorities are worried about the increase in the numbers of obese citizens. I presume instead of painting and decorating and digging and chopping in their quarter-acre blocks, they are chomping on Big Macs and from over-comfortable armchairs, watching the television or reading news media now mostly owned by Australians, Murdoch and the Fairfax corporation.

I hope, though, I can take you out of your armchairs, not only to allow you to throw the last of your Big Mac at me, but to ask you to share some of the love I have for New Zealand of the 1970s. A country that I was privileged to travel in from the North Cape to Invercargill, to be thrilled by mountains, hot pools and freezing cold lakes. To meet amazing people doing amazing things, which all reflected the spirit of those times and the unique character of a special country, with special values. Of course, now you have to watch out for those little people all over the place looking for a ring or something.

But back to the reason for this preface and the justification for a second edition of my book.

At the end of 1979 the principals of the little film company that had earned great respect and won prizes for its contribution to television, split up and went their separate ways. We had done as much as we could in television film terms really, influenced mostly by the lack of money around to support any further efforts. So, I went overseas trying to finance a film idea I had.

Hamdani also went overseas and, after becoming one of Hong Kong's most respected cinematographers, he formed his own video production company and has filmed throughout China, Asia and across the globe, for the BBC amongst others.

Hammond Peek continued with his sound-recording career and in the process picked up two Academy Awards.

I followed my star to the USA, England and Australia. I didn't manage to persuade Hollywood to finance my project so I turned again to writing, directing and producing for television in those countries.

However my television days ended through a disabling illness and whilst in Australia, recovering, my colleague Hamdani suddenly contacted me and a new partnership developed long distance. He learnt that I was writing again but when we discussed the sad state of conventional book publishing, he suggested I should self-publish and offered to help with the formatting and any other technical requirements whenever he had spare time between his work on video productions. So, with his help and encouragement - he even designed the covers - I published three works of fiction.

A new and exciting chapter opened up with my books also being made available on Kindle. Then when he called me to suggest that we re-publish *Hayes Over New Zealand,* I agreed that at this time, there really is a need for a nostalgic look at the best of the past. I was with Dr Seuss, who I'm sure would excuse my e-book versions.

Ever since the first edition, from time to time, folk have asked me where they could buy it. There seemed so few copies in the bookshops. Well the fact is that most of the stock was apparently lost when the publisher's store was flooded... something I learnt long after the fact.

So this final act has been for us to reproduce something of the original. I have re-read every page and re-lived the excitement and joy I experienced as a filmmaker in a very privileged situation. Also the text now will have fewer editing errors than were originally allowed to slip in. The photographs too have been improved and the self-published edition of *Hayes Over New Zealand,* in my humble opinion, is a far better product than the original ... I hope you will agree.

Hugh Hanafi Hayes

Foreword

WHEN I TOLD MY garage proprietor that I was selling up and moving from Christchurch, he looked hurt. Not because he'd be losing a major source of his income, from repairing my old car, no. His reaction became clear when I told him I was going to Auckland for a spell. Then he really expressed his feelings. "What are you going to that dump for?" were the last words he ever spoke to me.

Several years before that, when I was about to move house from Auckland to Christchurch, similar sentiments were declared to me by a colleague: "What on earth are you going down there for, you're too young to give up living!" I was told.

Then, even earlier, when I moved from Wellington to Auckland, all I got was a "Cheerio, be seein' ya."

Each time, I felt I was being reprimanded for my foolishness in moving out of the fold. For breaking up the family.

To understand the feeling, is to understand New Zealanders. They rarely rush to make a stranger welcome. Actually, they rarely rush to do anything. But once they size a body up and find they like him, he'll discover no stronger bond of friendship anywhere. That's if he's not pompous or arrogant. If he is, then it's a different story. He'll be "clobbered" and given a hard time for being "up himself".

Some commentators have complained that this attitude has created a culture of mediocrity and an unsophisticated, "grey", uninteresting people.

I think this book will prove otherwise.

Oh, sure the country's not the most sophisticated place on the world map. Although it certainly does try to keep up with many fashions: communist bosses in key trade unions, a top heavy public service and a high rate of unemployment. But the nation that produced Rutherford, Hillary, Inia Te Wiata and Luqman Hayes (my son), has other qualities that few can compete with.

For instance, could there be greater poetry than the atmosphere in the All Blacks' dressing room after a lost test match against Wales? Could there be a greater challenge to any man's intellect than trying to figure out the basic philosophies of New Zealand's political parties? Only geniuses could attempt to fathom the actual policies they espouse. Or can there be a more expressive way of showing one's gratitude or respect for another human being than with the Kiwi phrase "Good on yer"!

Unfortunately, the qualities of a nation are rarely appreciated at home. Indeed, I had to make a hazardous journey right across Canada and down the west coast of the United States before I could get the right perspective on my subject. Suffering the hardship of life in Sunny California, I was at last able to express my true feelings about the place I call home.

In a way, *Hayes over New Zealand* is an excuse to re-introduce my family. The family of people I met and came to know in the course of my many years as a reporter and filmmaker in that country. It's also an excuse for me to recall some personal experiences, from the most productive and fascinating period of my life so far.

From 1970 to 1978, I was fortunate enough to travel all over New Zealand many times, seeking the unusual to present in my programmes for television. During this time I met hosts of Kiwis, from all walks of life, who no one in their wildest fantasies could ever call dull and uninteresting. Many of these people and the things they did had such a profound effect on me that their lives and mine became inescapably connected. I thank Almighty God for my curiosity and a fair memory and I hope the reader will enjoy sharing both with me in the following pages.

H.H.

CHAPTER ONE

The Bard of the Bush

"DID YOU EVER THINK you'd like to have got married and settled down?" I asked the man.

His answer came without hesitation. Like a good comedian's when he picks up his cue from a feed:

"Ah, no, that was too much like dyin' to me. It's too bloody permanent. I didn't fancy that at all!" Blue-grey eyes twinkled and he scratched at his bushy red whiskers insistently, his hand practically disappearing in the hunt. "But my ole mate used to say to me, he used to say: 'Oh,' he said, 'all you want to be independent mate,' he says, 'is a good Swiss watch and a woman from anywhere.' But I never ever owned a good Swiss watch .... That's the ways he goes...."

The interview was over.

We both enjoyed the joke that day. So too, subsequently, did several thousand viewers, all over New Zealand. Then one of those minor miracles occurred, that fate produces from time to time. Suddenly, the joke was on the teller. That's the way she goes, all right.

Six months later, he'd lost his independence and the bulk of his beard. But he'd gained a wife. Yes, Overend Nelson, the gnarled and nutty Bard of the Bush, was wed. And virtually everyone in the South Island east coast town of Kaikoura danced at his wedding.

I didn't. Oh, I was invited to the festivities all right. In a way, I was responsible for bringing the couple together. However, I wasn't sure at that time whether I would be cursed or praised. Anyway, I had to get back to Christchurch. I had a film to edit: a precious postscript to a story that started earlier that year, on a back country farm in the Puhi Puhi valley.

That was where I first met Ovey and his equally hirsute

brother, John, in 1974. They were scrubcutters, working on contract to the local farmers, in the valleys of the seaward Kaikouras. They were the last of a dying breed in the district; men who cut and cleared by hand the densely thick manuka that cloaked the valley walls.

The brothers had worked in the area for twenty years, cutting and cursing their way through the tea-tree. For much of that time they worked with axe and slasher, until they finally put their trust in the whining chainsaw. It was still a tough job though, and they chose to make their life even tougher. The two men always insisted on living close to their work, in makeshift huts on the vast properties. With no mod cons and a constant fight with wild cats and opossums anxious to share their tucker.

But it wasn't the Nelsons' prowess with the chainsaw that had attracted me to the area. Nor, for that matter, their elemental lifestyle or their legendary drinking propensity. It was the poetry.

Ovey Nelson, son of a "Black" Irishman from Hawkes Bay, was no ordinary backwoodsman. A navy veteran from the Second World War, an army veteran from the Korean War and a tumbleweeding survivor of the freezing works carnage, Ovey was also a poet and philosopher.

His literary abilities came to my notice when I was still living and working in Auckland for the NZBC. That's an anagram for the BCNZ, the public broadcasting service that gets turned upside down every three years by the politicians. Unfortunately, like a bottle of wine, if you turn it upside down, it doesn't improve the taste. It merely brings the sediment to the top.

Anyway, I was just waiting to be transferred to Christchurch to a job with the pretentious title of Executive Producer, Current Affairs. I hoped it would give me the freedom to do the kind of television film work that I wanted to do. Not what someone else wanted. So I'd picked up a Christchurch paper, to see what was going on down there. After all, the South Island doesn't tend to crop up too often in everyday conversation in Auckland. In fact you could live your life in that city and never know there was a South Island. Let alone the Chathams and Stewart Island.

However, it was the south that was to provide me with so much fascinating material for filming. I was lucky to find many warm and interesting characters there. But the credit for finding the two most human stories I think I ever filmed goes to the Christchurch Star. Because it was in the Star, whilst still in Auckland, that I read of both Ovey Nelson, the poet-scrubcutter and Steven Roome, the little Christchurch boy born without arms. I filed them both for future reference.

I clearly remember the story of Ovey; it was in the sports and magazine section, with pictures and one of his poems. So he was a published poet. Actually, I was later given the original copy of that particular poem. It is called "On the Possum Trail":

> Out the back of Fort Apache
> There's lots of room to roam
> And in the thick manuka scrub
> The possum makes his home.
>
> But John is of another mind
> The old possum has to go
> He's got a swag of cyanide
> He says we'll make some dough.
>
> So come on you jolly scrubbies
> Get up the hill with me
> And never mind the billy
> There'll be no time for tea.
>
> Up amongst the heavy scrub
> The signs are everywhere
> John takes a draw on a cigarette
> And says we'll start right there.

With a tube of poison in his hand
And a grin from ear to ear
He grabs a couple of decent rocks
And gives them a mighty smear.

Onward, ever onward
Poisoning left and right
For he says that he is confident
There'll be a hundred here tonight.

All through the bush he's at it
Not passing a sign or clue
But by now we're getting buggard
And John says this will do.

The bait he's left about three days
Once more he's at the shack
He's got a brand new pocket knife
And a bloody woppin' pack.

And as we climb the rugged hill
The talk is of the yield
Till finally there before us
Stands the battle field.

The dead are strewn just everywhere
And we skin our fingers raw
A savage curse from John we hear
A good grey skin he's tore.

Forty or more the tally is
The day is almost gone
We both gaze upon the pack
And pass it onto John.

> Back at the camp the billy boils
> Then John is on his way
> Night settles at Fort Apache
> At the end of a skinning day.

The John referred to is Mr John Latter, a farmer who encouraged the brothers to indulge in a bit of hunting as a sideline.

Everyone in Kaikoura knew of Ovey's talent. Well they'd had poets amongst them before. Australia's Henry Lawson spent six months in 1897 just up the coast a few yards, teaching school. Apparently his wife had induced him to come to New Zealand to get away from his rollicking comrades in Melbourne. Good job Ovey and John Nelson weren't around in those days. She'd have grabbed her man and fled back to Melbourne for some peace and quiet.

Well everyone knows that the creative soul needs to let go sometime. It seems that every so often, after they'd spent a few weeks away in the bush, isolated and dry, the brothers would come into town for a week. But not to write poetry, by all accounts.

There's just too many other things to do in Kaikoura, even though the place has fewer than 2000 inhabitants. And that was before the National Government's emigration scheme started in the late seventies. Just the same, you see there's the "Adelphi", the "Commercial", the "Blue Pacific" and the "Pier". Not theatres, no. Pubs. So the boys always found plenty to do for a week.

Invariably, they stayed at one of the local motels. The one nearest to the hotel. At one time they used to bunk and breakfast in a caravan in the grounds of the motel. It was owned by the motel-keeper and placed at their disposal on a site even closer to the public bar than the regular units. They were almost twenty yards away. Their accommodation in town then was what I suppose could be advertised as "within staggering distance of the hotel bar".

Unfortunately, the grounds of the motel featured a fair

number of trees. The same kind of trees that lined the little sea resort's esplanade- Norfolk pines. Sturdy and attractive trees. Well that's what most people think. Certainly the motel owner must have; he had some really big, thick-trunked ones on his property.

A couple of them were between the pub and the caravan the Nelson brothers rented. Well they were until the night that John Nelson had an argument with one of them.

It was dark, you understand, and John had been enjoying the conviviality of the bar next door for a number of hours, I'm told, when it was time to go home. Apparently he was going well when he shot through the doorway on his way out of the pub, but before he could crash into the doorway of the caravan, he encountered this tall dark stranger. John went down. The Norfolk pine was unmarked.

Now John is the quieter of the two brothers normally. A little on the deaf side and a bit shyer than Ovey. But his shyness left him rapidly that night, when he was so unceremoniously felled, and his Irish pride filled the gap.

I'm not sure just how long it took him to get up off the ground and recover his balance. I should say get his balance really. Because the story I heard tells of a weaving, swaying, one-sided argument that took place between John and the inanimate bully. How long it lasted and at what pitch it ended, no one seems to know. But end it did, and abruptly. Apparently dumb insolence didn't satisfy John. He fetched his chainsaw. The next time he staggered from the bar to his bed, he wouldn't be clobbered by that one.

In the morning, the huge wooden corpse lay right across the motel lawn. Locals say it was a beautiful cut, considering it was done in the dark.

The noise must have been a bit worrying though. Around eleven o'clock on an autumn evening. But the motel owner was a most reasonable man. After all, the Nelson brothers had been good customers for many years. He'd had no reason to complain. Sure he had the motel's name and reputation to think of. It wasn't called the Norfolk Pines Motel for nothing.

But the customer comes first. At least that's what this proprietor thought. So he had the other tree felled. To save John the trouble.

Now the scrubbies had a clear run from the pub door to their caravan, with no unfriendly obstacles on the way.

Brother John wasn't home when I made my first call in person on the Nelsons. It was a research trip. I knew in my bones that a profile of Ovey Nelson would make a good documentary film. I'd pretty well known it, as I mentioned, from the time I'd seen the newspaper article.

By now I was living in Christchurch and producing a weekly film series called "Focus". It was basically a regional current affairs programme squeezed into fourteen minutes. However, I managed to stretch the meaning of current affairs to embrace human interest subjects as much as possible.

It was time to take a closer look at the bushman who wrote poetry. My researcher had made contact with the farmer he was working for at the time. His name was Des Keehan and his domain was about 3,000 acres of really steep, rough country in the Puhi Puhi Valley, about twelve kilometres inland from the coast.

Des was a bit of a character himself. All the farmers in the area were. The life is rugged, the hours long and the returns aren't exactly lucrative when you're farming on the slopes of mountains. But there's a strong sense of camaraderie amongst these hill people and a mischievous sense of fun. They pull each other's legs outrageously. Some of the yarns they spin would make even West Coasters envious. You really have to be on your guard. Their phlegmatic expressions can often fool you. If they can put one over a visiting townie, they've got something to chew on over the bar and roar at for hours. They're probably still laughing at my gullibility; I can be taken in fairly easily. However, I'm not so sure I would have swallowed the story that one of them pulled off on the Star reporter who wrote about Ovey.

The farmer, whose property the Nelsons were cutting on at the time, told the reporter that Ovey listened to the old tree stumps. According to the report, it was the scrubcutter's way of communicating with scrubbies of the past. The farmer assured the man that Ovey hears voices of the dead scrubbies telling him things to do. Like lay down his axe and chuck it in for the day. The paper printed the farmer's claim that he had seen Ovey listening with his ear close to a big old manuka stump.

Anyway he must have had his ear close to the ground on the day that we drove up to meet him. It was just after midday and the brothers had stopped cutting. The farmer and his son took us further into the valley and up to the siding where their hut was.

Outside the little wooden one-roomed shack, a body was stretched out full length on the grass. It had faded blue jeans and pointed brown shoes on its long thin legs. Above that a similarly faded jean jacket, buttoned halfway down, was topped by a cluster of gingery red hair and a battered felt trilby. The hat had been pulled forward to protect what little bare flesh there was on the face, from the sun. The arms were bent backwards to join up behind the head, cushioning it on its log pillow.

Mr Nelson was taking a post-prandial nap.

As we got out of the car, the body stirred, pushed the hat up onto the top of its head and squinted disbelievingly at the intrusion.

"What the hell are you up to Des? Some mischief, I'll wager."

It was a relief for him to recognise the farmer, I could tell. He kept his distance with my researcher and me, and related to us only through his friends at first. I was a bit worried. Perhaps it wasn't going to be so easy capturing this man and his character on film. Maybe he'd be too inhibited by strangers, let alone a camera poked in his face.

Slowly, though, he accepted us and his shyness dropped away. He called around the hut for his brother but got no answer. He couldn't understand it. John had been right there just a minute before, he said. "He must have took to his scrapers," he commented.

Ovey was about fifty-one, I guess, at this time, but he had the movements and wiry, tight physique of a man half his age. Only the etched furrows of his brow, the thinning hair on his head and the flecks of silver in his beard gave any sign of his age. He had a boyish sense of fun. In fact in my female researcher's company, he seemed to be moving about in the same awkward, springy way that teenagers do. His arms wrapped around his chest a little nervously. He'd be great, I concluded. Especially when he agreed to all my ideas for filming.

We left after less than a couple of hours, with the threat that we'd be back soon to record him for posterity. I called out to him to keep writing his poetry and we returned to Christchurch.

A few days later, I received a letter from Kaikoura. I feared the worst. Ovey must have had a change of heart. I am a professional pessimist when it comes to situations like this. Any circumstance that allows for the vaguest chance of my plans being wrecked means certain doom for me. If anything can go wrong, it will. At least that's what I convince myself before I ever really find out. I think it's a kind of self-protection instinct, so that when the blow falls, it doesn't hurt so much. If the blow doesn't come at all, then I've got a bonus. A bit like the guy who sits down to play cards saying: "I won't win."

My paranoia was completely unjustified. Ovey had kept his promise. Inside the envelope, was a poem. One just for me. It was handwritten of course, on a piece of lined exercise book paper. He called it "Attacked by NZBC" and here it is, just as he wrote it:

> It was windy in the gully
> Far too rough to cut
> So we shouldered up our saws
> And headed for the hut

We got home around midday
Cleaned and sharpened the saws
Fixed the bloody meat safe
And done some other chores

It was round about two o'clock
When up came a flash limosene
I knew it wasn't Norman Kirk
And I wasn't expecting the Queen

I wondered what had struck me
When it stopped outside the shack
For stone the bloody crows
There was Des and Kevin in the back

They got out and looked around
Des knocked em down to me
Then he ups and tells me
This here is the NZBC

Well they asked a lot of questions
What didn't mean much to me
A pretty weird sort of mob
This here NZBC

I looked around for John
Just to tell him they was there
But he had headed for the bush
Faster than a scalded hare

They were stiff, the fire was out
So I couldn't make a brew
And I don't reckon the little lady
Would have tackled the billy stew

After an hour or so of yarning
He said it was time he had to go
Just what the hell he accomplished
I guess I'll never know

They clambered back into the car
And he said he was comin back
He said next time I saw him
He'd have a camera on he's back

So if you're lookin at the square box
And a pair of whiskery barsteds you see
Don't take it out on the scrubbys
Go the bloody NZBC

Signed
Bard from the Bush

I couldn't wait to get him on film. But it had to be colour film. I insisted. Shooting that subject in black and white would be like eating caviar from an old newspaper.

At this time, the changeover from monochrome was at an inchoate stage in New Zealand. National network programming carried a bit of each, remember? Anyway, all priorities were for head office broadcasting in Wellington. In the meantime, the regions were expected to use up all the old black and white film stock. The irony of course was that it was the regional programmes that drew the audiences. So I fought for my little bit of colour film, and won.

We had three days only for the filming and that included all our travelling. That meant early starts and late finishes to get it done. The first part would fit in well with the Nelson brothers' routine anyway. They were up and away from the hut to start work each day at dawn. Just as soon as they'd swallowed Ovey's porridge and some liquid dynamite he euphemistically called tea. Ovey did all the cooking. Nothing too fancy of course, and always in a billy can or a camp oven. He didn't trust any of the more modern appliances, as he pointed out to me:

"Like, with that camp oven," he referred to an evil-looking, fire-blackened, iron vessel, "see, I can get a feed going on there and I can sorta tell when it's cookin' properly and if you leave the damn thing alone, you know it's all right. But with those electric stoves, if they're a notch too high or a notch too low, it either comes out raw or else ya can't eat it. You know, it's burnt or somethin'. I could never get 'em to match up at all, see, so... It wasn't so bad on those little ones. You know. A little one with just a switch on and off on it. You know, the element ones? They were all right. But these ones with these... I don't know what the hell they call it... automatics I suppose, you know. Things with clocks and things. I can't work them things."

Ovey had had a bad experience, I'd heard. On one farm where he was working, the farmer had made a serious mistake. It appears that the property couldn't supply an old hut for the brothers. There just wasn't one. The only thing the man could offer them to live in whilst they were cutting his bush, was a regular cottage. A simple, furnished, little house with such wonders of modern science as running water and electricity.

That didn't suit Ovey one bit. For a start he couldn't get used to the bed. It was a big iron thing with castors on the legs. The scrubby couldn't control it though. He complained to the farmer that it kept getting away from him. He reckoned he'd climb into the thing on one side of the room and wake up on the other side, practically out of the door. It had to go. Ovey liked to know where he was when he was asleep.

Then there was the stove. The electric stove with all the clocks and things. Apparently he had a terrible time trying to cook a hunk of mutton in the oven of the thing. He ended up sticking the meat into his faithful old camp oven, shoving that ugly utensil onto a shelf in the electric stove and lighting a wood fire under it. He wasn't going to let science beat him, that's for sure.

The morning light was breaking. The camera crew was finally happy. The colour temperature was right at last. The exposure sharp. The birds not too noisy. They'd got my assurance that they'd be paid overtime for working so early. So we started filming.

On the track, across the steep paddocks, where the sheep now enjoyed the space the brothers had provided, and up to the bush. The black and green, dense wall that fell to their chainsaws like dry grass to a sickle. Some of it forty feet high.

> On the hillside they stand
> The manuka I mean
> With grey twisted trunks
> And mantle of green
>
> Some may see beauty
> Where songbirds dwell
> But not the old scrubbies
> Of Geoff's Green Hell.

The first two stanzas of another little epic from the pen of Mr O. B. Nelson, Bushman, poet and philosopher. The philosophical side of Ovey coming out when we filmed him in his domestic setting, outside his shack.

We talked about his poetry. How in much of it he is throwing off about something or someone. In the nicest possible way of course. Indeed, the farmers of the district could pretty well bank on getting a missive in rhyme, pointing out a few home truths. These arrived in their postbox whenever the brothers had finished their contract and moved on to another farm. One farmer told me: "Ovey doesn't write poems for people, he writes them at people."

Most often, the verses carried a stinging comment about the very thing that provided him with his living. The bush. The manuka. Ovey explained his love-hate relationship with it like this:

"Well, I like it because it's kinda, well when I'm out there cuttin' wood, well see, nobody gonna come near me or bother me or anything. See, and I know when I reckon I've got me quota out I can turn round and come home (to his little hut, his wooden bench bed and his meat safe stuck up a tree outside) an' it don't matter if I dump old Des (the farmer) on the track or anything, see? See that's what I like about the job. See there's nobody says, well, you'll start now and knock off when I blow the whistle, see? That's the thing about it mor'n anything else. There's nobody standin' over you an' I think... I think the hardest boss you can work for is yer bloody self if y'ask me. Because y'know you may be inclined to try an' put it across the boss, but you won't put it across yourself, will ya? Y'have to get a quid if you can y'see."

The Nelsons must have made a quid all right in their time in the valleys. They reckoned to cut about an acre a day. At thirty-five dollars an acre. Not a massive sum to share between two. But if you're living simply, then it soon adds up. Indeed that was their style. "See, what I do is I go as long as I can on a job without gettin' any money and then when the job's finished, I get the thumper in one wad y'see."

Unfortunately, the wad didn't stay intact for too long:

"O, you'll bore into a bit of it that's for real, you know. You can guarantee you'll skittle a few quid in the pub. And then the horses'll have a go at some of it. And then there's usually a new chain to buy. Or I might have to buy a new saw. Or the old chariot might want fixin' up or somethin', you know, and that runs away with a couple of bob. Then you usually get stuck into the... the boozer takes a fair dollop of it. An' you get in there, an' the time you've gone, say you've had about a week off, you're that crook, you can hardly stand up. You're frightened to open the bin because there'll be nothing in it. You're thinkin', well, the best thing now I c'd do'd be to start all over again. That's about the guts of it."

I'm sure even Galbraith couldn't fault the economic validity of that conclusion. However I'm also sure he'd be academically horrified at Ovey's irresponsible disregard for the future. Here's the Kiwi bushman's thoughts on the subject:

"What's the use of planning? Can't do much planning, I don't think. I think it's only silly to plan. You could go an' save all your dough for the next three years in the scrub. You can go proper wowser. And you can walk down a street and get skittled with a truck, couldn'tya! Wouldn't be much fun in that. Oh, I think you gotta live for today, meself. Have a lot of fun. Then if you kick off, well what do you have to lose, anyway?" Ovey's broad smile parted his beard as his chainsaw had parted the manuka bush earlier that morning.

He was as innocent as the bush robins, fantails and tuis that gave him company when his whirring saw was at rest. I saw him serious only once. When I asked him if he believed in Divine Providence.

"Do you mean God?" He beautifully put down my pedantic phrasing. "Oh, yeah I do, yeah. You see... that's why nothing happens to me in the bush you see. God, I think is a bit of a nut for a bloomin' bushman, I think an', you know..."

"God looks after bushmen?" I suggested.

"I think so. Like you see, so many people say, oh you shouldn't back racehorses. But God damn it all, if God didn't want to see horses run he wouldn't have made 'em in the first place, would he. Eh? I don't see anything wrong with havin' a bet or two. I don't see anything heathen about that, do you?"

I assumed the question was rhetorical. I had no intention of debating it, that's for sure. On tape, for thousands to see and hear, Ovey Nelson was revealing a side of him that few I think had seen. Had been allowed to see. The fact is, not only was Ovey shy, but he had to be wary of most of the other human contacts he had. The farmers and locals. Great company and good friends, but invariably looking to pull each other's legs, as I mentioned. The scrubby never would have let his guard down with them. No way.

For some reason or other though, on this occasion Ovey felt

safe enough to speak out on personal things. I asked him if he prayed at all.

"I have done," he answered, picking at the scab of a thorn tear on his hand. "I'm not ashamed to say that. I think a lot of people have too that wouldn't let on. Oh, I think there's a fair bit of truth in it... Like, you take a guy... Man can make just about anything, but he can't make that tree or a bellbird or anythin'. And so there must be something... you know, man can't make those things... and they didn't just get there. I think God put them there all right. Though I can't understand what He was doin' when He put that lawyer (sharp, thorny vine) there. He must have been gettin' to the short end of His job when He got on to that stuff. He probably got that to annoy man, I suppose."

The farmer whose bush the Nelsons were decimating each day told me the main thing needed for their job was a big heart. Ovey didn't agree. He insisted that rather than a big heart, you had to be" about four pick handles between the eyes".

Well, however big-hearted or wooden-headed Mr O. B. Nelson was, at the time we filmed him he was certainly adamant about one thing. He was a very confirmed bachelor.

Back in Christchurch, I put the film together the following week. I called it "Green Hell" after Ovey's poem. It was shown to the Christchurch region a week after that. The little film was a first. The first regional documentary to be shot and transmitted in colour in New Zealand. Not that many people saw it in all its glory in those days. Most of us still had black and white sets, you'll recall.

The Nelson brothers saw it in colour though. I heard from a farmer that they'd joined the rest of the town in a local hostelry. Ovey was a brave man all right. Or else a born actor. Mind you, they would have been well fortified by the time the screen was filled with their fiery whiskers. I'm told the booze ran like a typical Kaikoura flood that night. I dread to think how many Norfolk pines went down in it.

The programme proved to be popular with everyone,

judging by the newspaper critics and the letters. It couldn't miss really. Ovey was made for television. He was the voice of individualism, the pioneer in all of us. The dinkum Kiwi, untouched by all the imported sophistication. A man of the bush. The guy we all become in our fantasies at weekends, when we're taming our quarter-acre sections.

A short while after it was screened in the south, the other centres in the North Island requested copies of the film. So Ovey was a national hero.

Then a couple of weeks after that, I received a letter. It was written by someone from somewhere in the middle of the North Island. An inquiry for information about Mr Nelson. The writer said that a relative had seen a programme about a bearded bushman named Ovey Nelson. The letter asked me to divulge his whereabouts.

Now, I'm a man of some ethics. I'd just made a film about the guy and I was still conscious of how lucky I'd been to get such a subject. It had done me no harm at all. In a way, too, I now considered the irascible bard of the bush as me mate, kinda thing. Well he really had that effect on you. So who was this person writing this demanding letter?

Maybe it was a wife he'd abandoned years ago and forgotten to mention. Maybe it was a debtor. Who knows what they wanted with poor Ovey? One thing was certain, I wasn't about to rat on him. Whatever he was wanted for. My secretary typed out the official answer.

"We are not at liberty to disclose the private whereabouts of persons who appear in programmes, etc..."

I'd forgotten all about the matter when the toll call came.

It was a woman, the writer of the letter. The request was repeated. Could I please help her to get in touch with Ovey Nelson, she wanted to know. "It's all right," she assured me, "I used to know him years ago. My husband has passed away now and I've been trying to find out where old Ovey is these days. It was a terrific surprise when I heard he'd been on TV... it said he was in the South Island somewhere."

I still couldn't be sure. But I could tell that the lady would persist until she got the information she was seeking. I decided to compromise. I gave her the address of one of the farmers in the valleys. I suggested she write to Ovey care of that address. She was satisfied.

Straight away, I contacted the farmer and explained what had taken place. My conscience was clear. Ovey had been protected. Well, he would be forewarned. I just hoped it would all fizzle out.

It didn't, of course. The next call came a couple of months later. The voice was phoning from Kaikoura. "Did you hear about old Ovey then?"

"No, what? What's happened?" I suddenly felt pangs of guilt.

"He's gettin' wedded on Thursday, thought you'd like to know."

"He's what?" I couldn't believe my ear.

"Gettin' married, it's right. At the post office in the afternoon. Are you comin' up?"

"You're pulling my leg, you devil!"

"Gospel, I swear it. Marryin' a lady he used to know when he lived up north. She's down here in Kaikoura now. They're stayin' at a buddy of Ovey's, 'til the weddin'."

I was still a bit wary, although it was beginning to make sense. What with the letter and phone call. My gosh, she really lost no time. She did mean business then, I thought. "But he told me that marriage was too much like dying, the old rascal. We had it on film."

"Well the little lady must have changed his mind. She's a lively one and that's for sure."

"What's this about the post office? What post office?"

"The Kaikoura Post Office. He's got to go there for the ceremony. See, the postmaster is the local registrar. He'll be lookin' after them, like."

It was all so bizarre, it must be true, I decided. Ovey Nelson, confirmed bachelor, whiskery old scrubcutter that he was, is the only person on earth that I could imagine getting married in a post office.

He'd probably get his car registration done at the same time! "I'm coming all right, what time is the ceremony? Where can I contact Ovey?"

I left Christchurch early on the day of the wedding. I'd arranged for a camera crew to fly up later. First, I wanted to check the scene out. To make sure they'd be welcome. Well at least that they wouldn't be abused. I couldn't be sure of anything with my old poet-scrubcutter any more.

My worries were quite unnecessary. Overend B. Nelson was as gracious in defeat as he had been while lying in the sun in the Puhi Puhi. He was attacking the contents of a bottle of whisky with some cronies when I called on him. Not in the pub, no, in the parlour of a friend's house in Kaikoura.

"Well, stone the bloody crows if it isn't Hanafi Bloody Hayes!" He was a little surprised to see me.

"Who put you up to this'n then? That bloody Des, I'll be bound. Come on in. Will ya have a snort?"

He introduced me in slightly slurred accents as "his old mate Hanafi" and I was enthusiastically accepted into the company. Mind you, I don't think a rabid bear would have been turned away, provided there was a spare glass to raise.

Ovey was already in his wedding suit. He'd probably been in it since dawn. Though he still had to put on a tie and stick his carnation in his buttonhole.

He looked a little different and it wasn't just the suit. The fungus had been trimmed. Ruthlessly. So the girlfriend had had the same idea as me. On the trip up from Christchurch, I'd bought a razor and a wooden rolling pin as wedding gifts for the couple. A subtle jape. I planned to present them on camera after the official ceremony.

"Will it be all right if we film the wedding ceremony, Ovey? A lot of people would love to share it."

"Oh, no... you're jokin'." He sounded like a man who had heard what he half expected to hear, but was half hoping he wouldn't. "I mighta known you'd have somethin' up your bloody sleeve... Surely you don't wanta take any more pictures of my ugly mug again. Bad enough seein' it on the box the last time... Whatja say Tom, eh? 'Ere take the bottle... This ere's the barsted from the N Z B C."

He pronounced the letters slowly and with purpose. Ovey was still as sharp as a ferret. He knew, even before he attempted it, that he could have made a horrible mess of that phrase if he'd tried it fast.

"You've got a lot of fans, Ovey. You can't let them down now. It's the love story of the decade," I teased.

He was grinning like a six-month-old baby.

"Seriously, Ovey," I put on my responsible, executive producer face. "Seriously, if you don't want us to film, just say the word and we won't. I'll have to phone Christchurch and cancel the camera crew, of course. That's if I can get them in time. They're flying up on a charter flight... I hope they haven't left yet."

I'm not really a rat, but this story was too good to be missed. The twist to the tale.

"No, it's OK on my account, I don't give a damn what ya do. But it's not just me ya see... is it? It's her's well. Daphne. You'll have to ask her if she minds ya buggerin' around with a camera an' everythin'. She might not like it at all."

"Where is she, now. I'd like to meet her anyway."

"Oh, she's away havin' her hair done. She'll be back soon an' yer can ask her yerself."

It wasn't long before I had the opportunity.

When she got back, I got the distinct feeling that Daphne wasn't exactly thrilled to see me sitting there. Not hostile, but just a trifle apprehensive, I would say. And she was stone sober.

An attractive woman in her late forties, the future Mrs Nelson gave me the impression that she wasn't about to let anything interfere with the day's business. She wasn't at all enthusiastic about the filming proposal at first, despite my assurances. However, she softened after I reminded her that but for the original programme this day's event may never have been possible. Nevertheless, she insisted that the actual ceremony in the post office couldn't be filmed.

It was a shame, but I had to defer to her wishes. The local postmaster would be disappointed. I'd already checked it out with him. Now he wouldn't be seen on camera.

With his crisply coiffured bride now out of the room, checking the arrangements, Ovey gave me a final message:

"See, it's her right, like. See, I don't care what ya say or anyone else come to that, but I love that woman... always have done since I know'd her..."

His hand was reaching for the bottle again when I left to meet my camera crew and sort out my filming. It was a simple item. A shot of Kaikoura, a flashback to his other programme, when he avowed he'd never get married, and a long shot from a hill of the little post office. I managed to get the voice of the postmaster reading the lines... "Do you, Overend Nelson, take this woman...", and I dubbed it over the exterior post office shot, with the little crowd gathered outside waiting.

Finally, I went down into the crowd with the camera and we caught the couple as they came out of the sorting section. The crowd cheered. I gave them the gifts and although it was a bit slurred, Ovey gave us a fairly rich parting shot: A bit too rich for the viewers, if I remember rightly. Then we were left standing in the confetti.

The last time I spoke to him, in 1979, Ovey and Daphne Nelson were still living in Kaikoura. He'd long since hung up his chainsaw and was working for the Ministry of Works. Oh yes, he'd been back to that post office again for another licence. He now had a dog, a golden labrador named - you've guessed it - "Whisky".

CHAPTER TWO

Capital Stories

Oh, capital city of hills and of dales,
Constantly tickled by 60 knot gales.
Your houses are white unless they are grey,
The concrete is rising to shadow the day,
Your harbour's inviting, for going away. H.H.

THERE WAS A CHAP walking down Lambton Quay (Wellington's most sophisticated shopping street) with a 12 foot long crocodile on a leash, when a police constable came along and stopped him.

"What's the idea?" the policeman asked, keeping a safe distance. "What are you walking along with that thing for?"

The man seemed a little surprised at being stopped. "Well," he explained, "I'm with an Australian circus, you see and we're just sightseeing."

The constable couldn't believe what he heard: "You're what? Don't you realise you're on a main thoroughfare? You'll frighten the wits out of pedestrians, walking along with that thing on a leash." He pulled himself up to his full 5' 8". "Take the confounded thing to the zoo!"

"Oh, sorry constable," the man said, "and thanks, I'll do that right away."

Well, a week goes by and the same policeman is on the same beat when, lo and behold, he sees the man again with the crocodile on a leash.

This time the constable isn't so tentative. He rushes up to the pair, very angry indeed:"! thought I told you a week ago to take that thing to the zoo," he explodes.

The man was smiling in recognition. "Yes", he said, "you did, officer."

"Well," yelled the constable, "what on earth are you doing

with it here now?" "Oh, well," says the man, "now we're going up to see the cable car."

The story may not be original, but it says a lot to me about the city that in 1865 became the nation's second choice as capital. Definitely not New Zealand's main tourist draw.

It's just as well, I suppose. Most of the time visitors can't get in unless they hang-glide. What with the Hutt Valley floods blocking one end and the south sealed off by strikes on the Cooks and Stewards Strait ferries, not to mention the airport closing down whenever there's heavy humidity. It's not easy.

But like the story says, the city does boast a zoo and a cable car for anyone who happens to get stranded in the district. It also has some quite colourful characters living there, as I have discovered over the years in jaunts around the place. Actually Wellingtonians, those that stay more than two years, have a good sense of humour. They have to have. How can you be serious about a town that builds its most prestigious office blocks right along an earthquake fault line? Including the Reserve Bank?

The humour, the very particular Wellington humour, manifests itself all over that city. Like the wall hoardings around the naughty part of Vivian Street, where the red light isn't a signal to stop. On a wall outside the Salvation Army buildings in that location, there was once a massive sign with the message: "I came that they might have life and that they may have life more abundantly." Then right next to it, another sign proclaimed: "Bargains here." I'm not sure just what was being sold there, by the way.

Mind you, not everyone expresses that debonair *élan*. As I found out quite early in my television career in the capital. There was an occasion when one of the nation's most distinguished daughters was in town. Miss Jean Batten, the first woman to fly solo from England to Australia and back was over for a visit.

Actually, this "spirit of the thirties" had lived in Britain for most of her life, so it was a rare visit. In television terms, she was considered "good value" for an interview. You know the sort of thing: "Do you think there have been many changes in aviation since your day... er excuse me, since you flew? Do you think those changes have been for the better for the solo flier? What changes do you envisage for the fliers of the future? Do you think those changes will be for the better?" and so on and on and on, *ad nauseam*. Remember when the screen was always full of those little gems of communication?

Anyway, in this case the lady herself wasn't too keen. She wasn't particularly interested in publicity as far as I could ascertain. It would require considerable charm and coaxing to get the dear lady to come to the party. I didn't think it was worth pursuing the matter, but my chief reporter at the time did.

When I got the assignment, I must admit I didn't know Jean Batten from a bar of soap. Not many of the New Zealand-born reporters did either. All the information I had was that she was a famous aviatrix, that she had been interviewed in Auckland already and was now in the capital somewhere.

I can't now remember clearly how, but after a lot of enquiries I finally tracked her down to the Convent of the Sisters of Mercy. She was sitting for a portrait by Sister Mary Lawrence, who was apparently a dab hand with the oils. I arranged to meet the flier there. Then I did some hurried research.

I'm not sure whether or not she was still posing for the painting when I arrived, but she was certainly posing. And playing hard to get. She is a very strong-willed little pilot, believe me. And very conscious of herself even though she was then on the wrong side of sixty.

Our first meeting wasn't easy. I didn't take to her really. Nevertheless, I had an assignment, and I gradually overcame her resistance, and with Sister Mary's help, managed to persuade her to be interviewed that afternoon in the studio. I shouldn't have bothered.

As soon as she arrived from make-up, she was frowning. At

the lights, at the cameras and at me. Then it started: "What lights are you using?"

I didn't realise what she was getting at. "Those up there!" I said confidently, pointing to the barrage of lamps suspended from the ceiling.

"Oh, that's no good, you can't just use those. That's what they did in Auckland. They made me look like an old woman." She was in a very agitated state. Twisting around in her chair and checking the monitor as the cameraman took up his position.

"What are you talking about?" I gently enquired. "They're the lights we use for everyone."

"I'm quite aware of that," she burst in. "But they aren't enough. Look at that - an imperious sweep indicated her image on the monitor screen - "see how hard and old I look?"

I called for the lighting man. She could let him have it, I decided. I just wanted to ask a few innocuous questions and go home. The interview was to be played in a magazine programme that evening.

The guy who had set the lights came in. I gleefully introduced him to her. Now Miss Batten had someone who could understand her problem from a technical point of view. It was quite a scene. She demanded he use more lights, beaming on her from several different positions. It couldn't be done, he explained. The lady was in a fury. "Well, I'm not going to be photographed looking like that. I'm sorry," she said, finally acknowledging my existence. "But I just can't allow the interview to take place... I don't want to be remembered looking like an old hag." And out she flew. The old aviator.

I'll always remember her. Just as she was.

But the uncooperative person was the exception rather than the rule generally. Indeed I was to meet a couple of real Wellington ladies later, who more than compensated for that experience. The first one wouldn't have minded if she'd been lit by torchlight.

She was a woman of seventy-one when I met her. A little

tenacious person, with frizzy hair and a heart as big as Ovey Nelson's. Her name was Sue Barcham. I found her quite by chance.

This was many years later, in 1975. I was making a series of programmes about New Zealand and New Zealanders, under the title of "One Man's View". Wellington was intended to be the subject of the second programme and I was in town to do some research before we started filming. At the time, I'd pretty well sorted out the theme of the film, the people who'd express it and the locations we'd shoot. There was just one outstanding thing I wanted to clarify.

My problem was whether or not to include any footage or comment on the motorway. It was a contentious issue and had been for some time. Environmentalists hated it. Homeowners feared it; four or five thousand people so far had been displaced. And the tombstones had to be moved for it. Even Edward Gibbon Wakefield, who'd lain in rest for years in the Bolton Street cemetery, had to shift. And he was one of the nation's most distinguished settlers.

Frankly, I didn't want to touch it with a bargepole. It was a heavy subject, whichever way you looked at it. I was planning a fairly light-hearted romp through the capital. The question was, could I afford to ignore the motorway? If not, how could I cover the issue, or even touch on it, without dragging the rest of the material down onto the floor?

Just about everyone I spoke to about the motorway talked as if they were on a religious crusade. It was the one thing in that city of incongruities that everyone was taking very seriously indeed. So I walked the streets, looking for inspiration. I looked down on it from bridges. I looked up at it from archways. I mooched around its edges and glared at it where it escaped underground. Nothing. It was just a hideously boring stream of concrete. I couldn't even think of anything comical to write about the gravestones being removed.

Finally, I decided to take a look at where the motorway was destined to emerge from the tunnel. It was in one of the parts of Wellington with the most character of all. Ghuznee Street, a cricket-ball throw from the Basin Reserve. And that's how I chanced upon Sue Barcham.

I was standing on the worksite of the motorway construction with my unit manager, a chap named Brian Walden. We were quizzing some workmen, trying to sniff out any odd little facet of information that could serve me, when we saw the birds. Hundreds of them wheeling in the sky right above our heads. All kinds of species were there, from pigeons to sparrows. Then, as some continued circling like planes over Kennedy airport, others flew down and took up positions in the little street opposite.

It was like the first day of the annual conference of the women's division of Federated Farmers. Except that these birds seemed to know instinctively where to perch. On the rooftop of an old grey-timbered cottage, among the branches and foliage of a huge tree in its garden and, like notes on sheet music, they settled row after row on the nearby telegraph wires.

"What the devil's this all about?" I asked a great burly guy in a yellow hard hat and a black singlet.

"Oh, they've come for a feed. It happens every afternoon at this time. The old lady, you'll see her in a moment, the old lady in that first house on this side, there, feeds them. You watch she'll be out soon. I reckon she's crackers."

We watched. Sure enough, just as the man had said, out of a little iron gate came a woman, carrying an armful of bowls of something. It was fascinating. As she crossed the narrow street of old wooden cottages, the birds came down to meet her. By the time she'd reached the kerb opposite her house, she was surrounded by hovering, diving, warbling, squabbling, pecking birds.

We were standing, half-hidden by earthmoving equipment, about twenty yards away. But it wouldn't have mattered if we'd been standing next to her. She wouldn't have seen us, so total was her concentration, so loving her attention, as she gently tossed handful after handful of grain and breadcrumbs to the insatiable sea of feathers, feet and beaks.

If she did this everyday, I wanted it on film. But exactly as I'd seen it. And I wanted to talk to the little old lady. She had to be a character. However, I had to be sure.

At this time, I was a stickler for spontaneity, if could get it. I've always hated the contrived interview. The set-up situation, where everyone walks to their marks and goes through a series of questions and answers that have been worked out and agreed to before. That method may elicit some information in a controlled way. It may save some film footage and sound tape. Invariably though, it produces dull television, rarely allowing anything of the personality of a person to come through. However well contrived and acted out it may be. I preferred to be as flexible as possible, to improvise and hope for the unpredictable. That way you have a chance of capturing the mood and character of a person.

It's not the average camera crew's ideal, of course. Some of them get into a terrible knot. Many have gone down fighting. There has to be a terrific cooperation between all parties: the cameraman, the sound recordist and the interviewer. The crew has to think on its feet and second guess both my movements and my intentions. If they don't, we all end up in a hopeless tangle, with the cameraman filming the soundman over my shoulder, picking his nose.

First then, the lady had to be approached. To get an idea of her personality. And to try to sense how she might react to being filmed and talked to. But someone else would have to do this. I wanted the lady of the birds to meet me for the first time when the camera was running. So I sat in a car, well clear, while my unit manager approached her.

He returned after about ten minutes or so with good news. The news I wanted to hear. The lady was lively, animated and colourful. She didn't mind one bit if we filmed her, and she understood that when we did turn up she would just carry on in her normal way.

A couple of days later we returned. At four o'clock, in time to film the arrival of the birds. They were the first players in the little scene. They arrived on cue. In ones, twos, and finally droves. Winging their way over the traffic of Willis Street, soaring down from the skyscrapers on the Terrace and skimming across the ugly clay gash that marked the ominous closeness of the motorway construction, at the bottom of the little street called Buller.

Again, just as when we'd first seen them, the birds took up their positions, waiting.

Then the star appeared. A little touch of rouge on her cheeks, her mousy hair pinned up as it was every day, her eyes bright and busy and her arms full of breadcrumbs and seed.

Down the little path she shuffled in carpet slippers and pinafore and out through the gate to the street. Completely preoccupied. We didn't exist. Yet we'd been filming her every movement from less than two yards away. She was a natural. The whole thing was done in one take. It turned out to be the most natural and spontaneous interview I had ever done. And it contained a bonus.

Mrs Barcham was halfway across the roadway, talking to her charges, tempting them down to her with the corn she sprayed into the gutter. But the birds wouldn't come. Something was wrong. The camera kept running.

"Well, they won't come down if there's people here." Her tone suggested she was more interested in the birds than meeting me right then.

There was just the slightest hiatus. Both of us were standing in the middle of the road, likely to be cut in half if a fast turning car had appeared. The cameraman was frantically searching along the gutter for signs of a bird. Whilst above us, like spectators in a Roman amphitheatre, a hundred feathered prima donnas watched our every move.

"Shall we go across the road and have a chat then?" I decided it would be safer to talk outside her house. Also our withdrawal might give the birds some confidence.

Now someone else had joined the scene. A black cat had stolen past and was lurking by the gutter. Obviously he was as anxious as I was that the birds should descend for their meal.

Sue Barcham turned on it sharply: "Blackie! You've been fed." The cat retreated sourly.

I had walked back to the path. Again I called her: "Will you come over here? Can I have a wee talk with you?"

She emptied out the contents of her bowls along the footpath and gutter opposite. "Yes," she said, finally and reluctantly turning from her friends and shuffling to safety.

"Are they your birds?" I asked, once she'd negotiated the kerb without losing her loose carpet slippers.

"Well they are now (chuckle). Well I say they belong to me if anybody touches them," she answered defiantly.

Slowly their greed overcame their fear and the birds flew down.

"How long have you been doing this routine then?" We were now just a couple of people, standing on a street corner, having a chat. The cameraman, with the camera on his shoulder, was shooting free range.

"Well, I've been feeding the sparrows since 1968. And then um, well the odd pigeon was coming up and the sparrow... it wasn't like this." The path, kerb and gutter across the road was now a moving mass of bird life. "And then, um, you know, I'm getting a bit more bread each day..."

Her voice ended with an upturned intonation. She'd made her statement end as if she was reminding herself of the fact. Indeed, her whole speech pattern was full of flavour. Not at all the usual monotone of much New Zealand speech. There was a wealth of vocal variety that made her so interesting to listen to.

"...you see, they've told all their relations."

"I should think they have. Just about every bird in Wellington's here."

"Well, you know animals communicate."

"Do they?"

"Oh yes, and so do birds, they all communicate."

"Well, how do birds communicate then?"

"Well they've got their own way of communicating, I mean I read books on them."

I wasn't going to let her get away with that answer. She'd sidestepped more adroitly than a politician.

"Well, do they say 'there's a load of bread going down that road'?" That should get an answer I thought. I was wrong. She ignored the bait completely.

"You see, and of course I've got to buy two loaves of bread a day, and 3lb of wheat and 3lb of barley."

"You can't get a farm subsidy, can you?" I questioned.

"No, I don't think so," she was dead serious.

"It must cost you a fortune, does it?"

"It does, with feeding twenty cats!"

I wasn't expecting that one. "Twenty cats as well? Where are they? Indoors?"

Mrs Barcham looked around at the house behind her: "There's six indoors. They're all around here. They're all strays," she added affectionately.

"Well, don't the cats go for the birds?"

Her answer was definite: "No, they've been taught not to."

"Have they? How did you teach them then?"

"They know what NO means," she pronounced the word with real emphasis. "And on the odd occasion, I've taken my belt off and given them a little tap." She smiled.

"Have you?"

Sue gave us a little demonstration, miming a strap in one hand and pointing a finger with the other: "No, you mustn't, no, no, no. And they know they mustn't touch the birds."

I wasn't totally convinced that the cats fully understood the old lady's gentle admonitions. Or that they always bothered to acknowledge them. Blackie, the one who'd been ordered away from the scene earlier, was sliding along the fence opposite right then. His narrowing eyes were watching a veritable orgy of feathers and flesh hopping about. Then again, maybe her presence with me was stopping the cat from making his leap.

"What about the dogs?" I had to ask the question. A big old

gingery hound had sidled up to us from nowhere. I knew he was on camera. His timing was immaculate.

"Well, he's the odd one that loves me," she took it in her stride. "He comes down for the odd feed every day."

"Well," I joked, shoving his too friendly head away, "what's his feed, the cats?"

She was adamant: "He doesn't touch the cats, they chase him."

"I've never known such disciplined animals."

Sue Barcham was in her element. "Oh well, of course... and if it's raining I won't allow them outside in the wet. They go to the door and I say 'No, you can't go out, it's raining,' and oh, they run back. They do as they're told..."

She was cut off then by the sound and fury of a big old car screaming down the road with tyres squealing and exhaust unmuffled. The birds flew up in a cloud. "Now that's the sort of car that runs over the pigeons." She was furious. "I went out on the road one night and there were three dead."

I chose to change the subject: "What do the neighbours think of all this?" It was a good choice.

"Oh, well, of course, I've been crucified by most of the neighbours."

"Have you?"

"Oh, yes. Well they teach their kids to throw stones at the birds."

"Do they?"

"Oh yes. And even the grown-ups would throw stones at the birds because... I don't know. They just don't like me feeding the birds. So of course, I call it 'Six months of the battle of the birds'." She was really warming up to her subject now. I'd stumbled on a sore spot, it seemed.

"Six months?" I prompted. "Yes, the battle of the birds, and of course I used a few swear words at the children."

"Did you used to throw stones, then?"

"Well, I told one man that if he threw any more stones, I would stay up all night and pitch some on his roof. Because I wasn't going to have my birds, ah, tortured." Her turn of phrase was beautiful.

"Tortured?" I repeated.

"Tortured," she insisted.

The corrugated iron roof of the cottage across the street was obviously the one she was referring to. It was a favourite perch for thousands of birds, I would think. I don't know what colour the original tin was painted, but at that time it was a mottled, crusty off-white and brown. Her stones, had she carried out her threat, would never have penetrated.

"What about when all these birds are satisfied? They leave little droppings, messages, don't they?" I was nodding towards the ornithological clearing station opposite.

"Well, of course, the houses are that old it doesn't matter," she answered disdainfully.

"No?"

"And all these houses were going to be pulled down."

My ears pricked up. "Are they?"

"They were."

"They were? What do you mean, they were?"

"Well they've suddenly decided they're going to save that side" (where the birds exercise their rights) "but they're going to take my side."

I sensed blood. "Is this for the motorway thing?" I asked, casually.

"Yes." The single word encompassed a multitude of feelings. I had to be careful.

"Well, they'll never do that, will they?" I tried to sound as ingenuous as possible.

"Well, of course, not to me they won't. I'm the only one that hasn't sold."

"You're staying here?"

"Oh, well of course, they'll have to drag me out boots and all." Sue Barcham was magnificent. I had to go on.

"Will they?" She needed little prompting. "Oh, yes, I've got twenty cats to think about."

"Well," I suggested, "you can set the cats onto them, can't you?"

The lady snorted. "Well, of course, I don't have to set the cats on them. I'm quite capable of looking after meself, really." I didn't doubt it for one minute.

Now I had my motorway story. And just the angle I would have wished for. The human tragedy, when the feelings of people have to be sacrificed for concrete, at the whim of insensitive, faceless town planners and ambitious politicians. The environmentalists would love it, I knew. Just one more touch though, just to make sure.

"Yes, but are they ever going to build that motorway? I mean, nobody seems to know where it's going."

No scriptwriter could have given me a better answer: "They make you sick," she scoffed. "Of course I've told them all to go to blazes. I mean, I just won't. I'm not going to give up my life." The last word was almost a plea. "I'm seventy-one. I'm not going to give up my life."

"No, why should you?" I encouraged.

"No."

The topic was closed. She'd have more to say, no doubt, when the day of judgment came. Or when the Ministry of Works moved in with the bulldozer. Whichever came first. In the meantime, I returned briefly to the subject we'd started with.

"Why do you think you like birds so much?" It was an obvious question in the circumstances. But the answer surprised me.

"Well, er, the thing is I've always craved for love and affection. And I've missed out." She said it without any kind of emotion.

"Have you?" "Yes. And I think that being involved with birds, animals cats, dogs, anything... lions if you like... I get it back a hundredfold."

"You wouldn't go out and feed a lot of lions would you?"

"Yes, I would. I would like to live up at the zoo. But then I wouldn't be able to feed me birds."

Little Sue Barcham meant every word she said. I know that for a fact. Her dedication to birds and animals was profound.

She even refused to go away on holidays after the birds started arriving, because she couldn't get a bird sitter. Seriously, if ever she wished to go out and tried to get someone to do the feeding, she was refused. But the birds never were. When her grandson got married way over at Titahi Bay, the determined old lady left the reception, went home, fed the birds, and then went back again. She felt she had no choice, even though the journey took about an hour or more each way.

Apparently she excused herself after the wedding breakfast, saying: "Well I'm not going to let my birds starve, not even for one night. Because I'm eating, why shouldn't they?"

I've no idea what the family thought of her that night. Or for that matter all the time. I did meet her husband, briefly. He was almost a shadow in the background. Totally deaf. Sue told me that he wouldn't have anything to do with the birds or the cats.

I called round to see her in 1979, on another visit to the city with a zoo and a cable car. They must have dragged her out, boots and all. The house and the street were gone. And so were the birds.

I don't think the other lady I met and filmed in Wellington had ever left a wedding breakfast to feed birds. For one thing, nothing as common as a sparrow ever ventured where she lived. She was a lady of Karori, the cummerbund district of the capital.

My intrepid little researcher, Jan Crocker, discovered her by devious means, to fill the role of the "hostess with the mostest".

You see, I felt that with all the various embassies and clutches of diplomatic corps located in the capital, there must be a vibrant and fascinating social scene. You know, gay, sophisticated parties with Corban's champagne fizzing over and dripping carelessly onto the broadloom.

Maybe it's my plebeian background, I don't know, but I've

always had a hankering to know what goes on in the big houses where the wealthy live. I'm sure the curiosity is quite natural. Conversely, I imagine that the people who live in big, wealthy homes are constantly wondering how it is for us others. I bet they would love to peek in on a typical scene where a family of eight are living in a three bedroom, 1,200 square feet residence.

Well on this occasion, I didn't think any programme I was making on Wellington would be complete without including at least a taste of that slice of society. I needed a representative therefore. A hostess who had entertained in the grand manner and who would tell me all, in phrases dripping with superlatives. Well, we didn't quite make that. But we did have a most charming Karori housewife, who was prepared to let us into her home with the camera. She would have been furious if we'd turned up without it in fact.

Our choice was an unashamed snob. A Wellington snob. Her name was... well, let's call her Antoinette Marie, wife of a chartered accountant in the city.

Wellington, I had always considered to be the least parochial of New Zealand's cities. That is until I met madam. Then I got a flavour of a different attitude. The conviction that it is indeed the nation's cultural centre. I'd never thought of it that way. Oh, sure the RSA always holds its annual conference in the Wellington Town Hall and there's a pie cart outside the railway station most nights, but that's not all, according to the lady from Karori.

She claimed it was full of the most interesting people in New Zealand. And if that were not enough, her feelings for Auckland were summed up in the contempt she expressed for that city's lack of interest in a recent sale of Picasso etchings. Apparently they were a limited edition and therefore of high value. It seems that Wellingtonians bought the lot.

Her framed copy was lying casually on the *chaise longue* when I entered the sitting room. My first *faux pas* was to refer to it as a lounge. But the lady was most forgiving. After all, I had shown interest in her collection of paintings hung on the walls of her exquisitely white and pastel hallway. Not a chip or finger mark to be seen, I noticed. The chandelier would be worth a bob or two also.

Antoinette Marie was a delightful, vivacious hostess from the moment she showed me a self-portrait by an artist she knew and whom she expected me to know. "What do you think of that, my dear?" Her accent couldn't have been improved even at Roedene, England's top private school for girls. "That's a self-portrait painted by the artist herself."

"Oh, a self-portrait, painted by herself!" I repeated, impressed. The repartee was scintillating.

"That's cute," I mumbled as I picked up a box of matches from the top of an antique sideboard. The box bore the family name in gold script, on a deep blue background that matched the drapes at the bay window.

"Yes, we think so," she fluttered. I had held the box up to the curtaining and quipped: "They match!" but it was wasted. She was obviously on a different level.

"But of course, my dear. Do sit down and feel comfortable."

My hostess was an attractive, blonde-haired woman in her forties. On this particular day, she was garbed in a purple chiffon harem suit, with a spare piece of material wrapped around her neck and thrown over her shoulders. She wore matching glasses. From time to time that is. Not when the camera was on though, I noticed. Then she was sheer elegance, draped full length on the *chaise longue*, with her feet pointing directly at me.

I was sitting on a slightly uncomfortable and extremely expensive antique armchair, with a hard cushion rammed into my back, trying to look relaxed. It was too much though. I found it impossible to carry out an interview in the right mood while I was sharing a chair with a massive block of flock. I pulled it out from behind me, excusing myself as I did so. She was charity itself.

"I suppose it's not the done thing," I suggested, "to show one's discomfort in a host's chair?"

"Oh, don't be silly, not at all, just toss the wretched thing over there. We don't stand on ceremony here, my dear. Feel free to do what you like. We've had all sorts of people in this room, sitting on the floor and everywhere."

"Nevertheless, you would tend more to the caviar than say the pie, wouldn't you?"

"Well, yes, you might say that, but only because if I were giving a party say, I'd have to make the pies and I can buy the caviar." The answer was obvious. "But you haven't said anything about my Picasso, my dear," she swept on. "Isn't it absolutely gorgeous? I just adore it, don't you?"

The etching had been moved from the *chaise longue* to make room for Antoinette's feet. It was now lying, propped up at an angle, on the priceless table by my right arm. I couldn't miss seeing it. At least I was meant not to.

"Oh, yes, it's charming. Done by the artist himself, I suppose?" She ignored it. "My dear husband bought it for me, isn't he a darling? What would you say if the man in your life bought you a Picasso etching instead of a washing machine?" I decided the implication was innocent and unintentional, so I just answered the question.

"Well, it would depend, if I wanted to wash some socks..."

My answer was tossed aside for the mundaneness it expressed.

"Well who wants to waste time washing for heaven's sake, when there are so many beautiful things to see."

"The little tea set is beautiful," I mentioned, reminding her that she'd previously made tea for us in her very special bone china. Fragile little cups and saucers, with scenes of Wellington on them, clustered round a delicate teapot.

"Oh, yes, I'm glad you reminded me." She eased herself gracefully into a sitting position and poured.

"The tea is cold," I blundered out, forgetting for the moment where I was. My hostess wasn't disturbed one bit. "Of course the tea is cold, but the hospitality is very, very warm, my dear." Tallulah Bankhead couldn't have delivered the line better if she'd tried.

The *tête à tête* was most enjoyable. I could almost feel my unit manager stifling his laughter in the background. However, I hadn't really discovered what I'd come for. Oh, sure the film would show the beautifully furnished and tastefully designed interior of a Karori home. But what of the lifestyle these gentlefolk must enjoy?

To introduce this part of my programme, I had already filmed the exterior of Government House. The terraces and endless windows of that sedate seat had been the background to a question I'd posed on camera: "I wonder what kind of people get invited here?"

"You've been to dinner at Government House, of course?"

"Yes, I have. No, it was a luncheon. I beg your pardon, a luncheon, yes."

"Well, I was wondering if they're still very lavish. Or if they're taking into account the economic situation, you know."

"Well, it may not be lavish, but the food's always very good at G. H."

"They're not serving up baked bean sandwiches or pies yet then... things are still..." I wasn't allowed to finish the sentence.

"Why must you insist on pies for heaven's sake? My dear, one doesn't go to Government House just for the food, anyway. One goes there for the interesting people one meets and what they can contribute. For instance, when I was last there, I had a writer on one side of me and a Bishop on the other... now, isn't that interesting?"

"You wouldn't meet a window cleaner there though would you?"

"Certainly not" she flashed back. "Because he wouldn't have anything to contribute..." She was delightful, Antoinette Marie. A veritable champion of the upper dog. And life was just a beautiful series of wonderful little gatherings with terribly clever people. At parties. In the local drama club that performed in the grounds of the British High Commissioner's residence. Their plays I mean. And not forgetting luncheon at jolly old G. H. of course.

But she was wrong about window cleaners. I knew just the man to tell her so, too. His name was Mr Harry James Henry Downs and he was attendant in charge of the Carillon Tower and the Hall of Memories on Wellington's Mt Cook. He cleaned the windows there, amongst his other duties. But not in the conventional way, atop a ladder, or slung precariously from a cradle. No, Harry had his own way, particularly for the high ones in the war memorial chamber.

In order to wash the glass, he used a discarded government flag pole with a mop end, over which he laid a piece of chamois leather. For the general dusting in those regions, he had another long pole with a broom tied to the end. That extended to about sixteen feet. Then to get even greater elevation, Harry used to stand on an empty lemonade crate.

He was up on the crate, cleaning, when I first met him.

A brisk, agile little man with wispy grey hair and horn-rimmed glasses, Harry Downs was a credit to his uniform. Even though it was a shade too big for his slight frame. Never mind, in that slight frame was another great ambassador for Wellington, despite the fact that he had been born in London in 1911. However, his heart and taxes had long belonged to Godzone and he was a great ambassador for New Zealand too.

Harry cleaned and cared for the nation's shrine to the fallen in war, with dedication and pride. Each day before the building was open to the public gaze and the soles of their feet, he spent an hour-and-a-half cleaning.

When I asked him how he came to get such a job, his answer was a forewarning of one of his very definite personality traits: "Well, I'm afraid I'm one of those individuals that sort of takes things literally. My father's advice, when I was a very young man, was to ensure that I earn my living the clean way. So that is how it comes about that I've had this job pretty well all my life."

That's right. Harry was a punster, and a talker of nonsense in order to work in one of those atrocious plays on words. He also delivered all his conversation in the same, recitative style he employed when lecturing the public on the wee guided tour he conducted. Mind you, he knew all the answers; every symbol and meaning behind all the sculpture and murals in the place. Unfortunately, he had all the information lodged in his memory in a set order. If you interrupted his spiel, he had to stop and go back to the beginning again.

But he was a great entertainer. The puns were the worst part. He actually knew some pretty good jokes. In fact he didn't stop cracking them all the time we were in the place: in the sacred shrine, up the stairway, on the elevator, around the platforms of the bell towers, everywhere. He loved an audience and we made a fatal mistake. We laughed at his first joke.

It smacked of his past, I think. Harry had been a seaman. He was in the merchant navy before and after he came to New Zealand in 1936. Indeed he didn't settle permanently on dry land until the 1960s. You may have heard it, the joke, but it's still very relevant.

"There were these two surgeons, you see, who hadn't seen each other since leaving medical school. Well one day, they met up again and this was the resulting conversation:

'Hello, Charlie, how are you today? What are you doing in the profession?' 'Oh,' says Charlie, 'I took up appendectomy. It's quite an easy way of earning a living. Just a matter of snip, snip and Bob's your uncle. What about you, Fred?'

'Oh,' says Fred, 'I'm in the sex change business, you know. Just a matter of snip, snip and Bob's your auntie!' "

And if you think that's dreadful, you should have heard the puns. For instance at the top of the bell tower, he dispensed these beauties in his best tour conductor's tones:

"At the top of the tower, in the main belfry there are forty-seven bells with a total weight of thirty tons. That's thirty all told (tolled)." Ouch!

"What about all the pigeons up in the top? Are they a nuisance?" "Oh, no," says Harry. "They like to nest there.

They are hoping that if they lay their eggs up there, they'll turn into bellbirds," (pause) "but sometimes they drop down and when an egg lands on my shoulder, I can't help but think that the yoke is well and truly on me."

Whoever said interviewing old characters for television is an easy job? Or odd characters.

The oddest one I ever met was also in Wellington. A man who couldn't help but fascinate. However I couldn't get him on to film. Well, not with his cooperation and blessing, that is. I could have filmed him in action with a telescopic lens, I suppose. Then again, his particular activity of interest took place between dawn and sunrise and that makes it difficult for the candid camera.

Actually this one lived in Eastbourne, to be precise. That's where the penguins gather in winter and the English gather all the time.

This chap, though, was neither a penguin nor an Englishman. He was Dutch, and naturally enough, for a son of the land of windmills, his interest was in power and producing energy. He was an inventor. Invariably of things that moved. I believe he was inspired in this direction originally when he worked as a door-to-door brush salesman. Rather than drag a heavy caseload of products by hand, he designed a little pram or trolley to carry his wares. It hooked on the back of his bike.

But the man was destined for a much more significant role in the future of humanity. At least that's what he thought. Well, he was around forty then, so he still had time.

The Dutchman lived in a small house, perched on a hillside. The house was very humbly furnished but full of books and religious tracts. I believe he was convinced that the inspiration for much of his work came from above. I wouldn't like to argue. For one thing, I didn't get a chance to take a look up in the loft.

But I was privileged to see him in action on one of his proudest inventions. A unique method for propelling oneself in a forward direction. The last part is important. You see the guy believed that it was essential to design any form of vehicle to go forward only. This conviction was based, if I understood correctly, on the hypothesis that man was a forward-moving creature. His argument was that going backwards was therefore not only alien to man's nature and contrary to his physiological abilities, but it also wasted energy. Power. I was going to add that it can also be quite dangerous, especially at speed downhill. But I didn't want to spoil my chances of seeing his invention.

All was well. He put it on for me. Or rather he climbed up and into it. No, on to it. Well, both really.

I don't think he had a name for it at the time, and frankly I find it very difficult to describe it. Or them. Yes, I suppose correctly speaking, it was a them. Two things that make a whole. And they fitted on the legs. No, that's not right either. The legs fitted into and on them. The main part of each of them was a wheel about ten inches in diameter. Above each wheel, and free of the rim of course, was a steel platform just big enough for each foot. Then each of those bits was in turn connected to a couple of padded leg braces. These, if I remember correctly, fitted up the back of each leg as far as the thigh. In other words, the legs remained unbent and were strapped into the braces.

Now in order to get into and up on these, you needed a couple of solid gate posts to haul yourself up by. And a damn good sense of balance when you got there. Ten inches above the ground remember. Anyway, once he was up there, I could see how the thing was mechanically operated. The two plates were like accelerator plates in a car. When he depressed each one, by pushing down with the foot, it motivated a series of rods that turned the wheel. A bit like the action of a train wheel.

That was it, basically. Except that the power derived from the action of the feet wasn't used only to drive the wheels round. No sir, there was also a small dynamo which in turn powered a small rear light. Ingenious. Once you got going that is.

But starting and stopping both had their worrying moments. Especially stopping. There was no braking system, you see. In fact, the whole device (or devices) was (or were) designed, as the inventor said, for forward movement. Indeed, even the accoutrements that he wore or employed to assist him aided that intention.

For one thing, he wore a crash helmet with a rear view mirror connected to the top. Then, once he was moving, he harnessed the aid of any following wind with what looked to me like two table tennis bats.

He was something to behold, believe me. But if you don't have a private demonstration, you've got to get up early in the morning to catch that boy. Some have. In dawn's early light. Once the town had got over its initial terror and figured out what the strange thing was that zoomed along the promenade each morning.

I'd like to have shared this sight and philosophy with all New Zealanders, but sadly the chap refused to allow us to film him. He wanted us to wait until he could show us something really interesting. And important. Something he was working on at the time in his shed. It was, of course, intriguing. Especially since the little wooden structure on his section defied our inspection. I put a man on it whilst our friend was pedalling or whatever he did on his wheels. The workshop was boarded at the window and padlocked at the door, I was told. So his secret was safe.

However, he told us enough to whet our appetite. This was in 1975 remember. The Dutchman said that because the natural sources of power would run out soon, he had studied the whole subject of power and mobility. He'd also had informative dreams about it. Soon he would be able to reveal the answer. The solution to creating perpetual power and energy. It would save the world millions. Indeed it would save the world. And it was all in his little shed.

CHAPTER THREE

Up North... For A While

IT'S HARD TO UNDERSTAND, sometimes, why so much fuss is made by Maoris about being deprived of, or sold short on their land.

Now don't get me wrong. I'm not about to enter the debate over rightful ownership, or who was here first and all that nonsense. I'm simply talking about value for money, in terms of bartering.

Take the city of Auckland, for instance.

As I understand it, Governor Hobson's boys paid the equivalent of fifty-five pounds sterling in gold for the place. Not to mention all the blankets, clothes, pots and pans, tobacco, flour and sugar that was included in the transaction. And that was before even Smith and Caughey's department store had been built.

You just imagine what that little lot would be worth today, if it had been salted away prudently. The gold alone would have a value of around $40,000. Throw in the cost of a bag of sugar at current prices, and you realise that the Maori landlords didn't get such a bad deal after all. Especially when you consider the place is just a giant anthill anyway.

Mind you, it's very fertile land. No one can deny that. When I lived there, I used to get an amazing crop of mildew in my shoes if I left them in a closet for more than a week. I wasn't the only one either. I remember a cameraman getting quite a shock. This guy lived on the North Shore. He hadn't long moved up to the area from Christchurch and was completely unaware of the climatic difference between the two centres. It seems that he was planning to take his wife out for a treat. They were going to a special function that required them to wear formal dress. You know, monkey suit, bow tie and his hair combed for a change.

Anyway, on the evening of the "do", while his wife was gliding gracefully into her beautiful new gown, the cameraman opened up the cupboard to get his tuxedo out. That's when he got the shock. Instead of finding the conventional, black dinner suit he'd put in there, he discovered a green one. The outfit was covered in mildew. Of course, these days green dinner jackets are all the rage. Maybe he was the fellow who started the fashion.

Actually, I'm very fond of Auckland, despite the ants and the fungus. For one thing, any city that can name one of its streets after a British military failure in India (Khyber Pass) has got to have a sense of the bizarre. For another thing, the younger of my two sons was born there and that was a blessing.

It was also, for me, a great place to learn my craft in television broadcasting. There seemed to be lots of scope for both the serious and the absurd, in terms of subject material. The only problem was that it was difficult at times to sort out which was which.

I do have one regret though. Of all the stories I covered or concocted over the years, particularly in the north, I never managed to come up with a Maori "character". To feature in a film, I mean. Or for that matter, a Polynesian "character". That's surprising really, when you consider that Auckland has such a large non-European population. Oh, I met and filmed plenty of Maoris all right. From proud and distrustful shack dwellers in Northland, to Stewart Islanders as white as the driven snow, who claim Maori ancestral rights to the annual mutton bird massacre.

Maybe I'm just unlucky, but as a reporter or filmmaker, all the stories I did relating to Maoris were either pretty heavy, or at best fairly earnest. And yet I know that their true nature is very light-hearted and full of fun. It's a paradox. I suppose the fun and enjoyment of life is still exclusive. It can only be expressed in a family group context. On the marae, for instance, or in peer groups in other situations. I don't know. I'm sure, however, that a bright anthropologist like Rangi

Walker would know.

I mention Dr Walker because he was, in fact, the very first person of any race that I interviewed for television in Auckland. The interview took place on the flat rooftop of the then highest building in Otara. We were up there for the view.

It was a depressing sight. A massive State concentration camp. A vast economic ghetto, designed to concentrate one section of society in a spot that everyone else could easily avoid.

This was in the early days. When Otara was treeless, grassless, arid. And Rangi Walker hadn't come up there to joke about it, I can tell you. Indeed, he'd just obtained his doctorate with a thesis on the very subject we surveyed from that roof. It wasn't the lightest interview I would ever do, and Rangi was certainly not in the Ovey Nelson class as a character.

Nor for that matter was Harry Dansey, the late race relations conciliator. Yet Mr Dansey was a fine journalist, a marvellous raconteur and a damn nice person. For me though, he just wasn't eccentric enough. No, the nearest I came to finding my Maori "character" was in Taupo.

I was in that town once to do some magazine items for a television programme called "This Day". My visit was what was called an "away trip". What that meant in reality was that instead of sitting in a newsroom in Auckland waiting for stories to come in, a reporter went on safari to find some. With a camera crew. Nothing was pre-planned, apart from the motel bookings. You relied on your nose, your ears, your eyes and the local newspaper editor.

Sometimes the mission turned out to be quite fruitful. You might be lucky and come up with two or three happenings or oddities that would make reasonable items. Sometimes you would scratch around for days desperately searching. Never would you return empty handed. And always the camera crew would be bored out of their minds. Or make sure you got that impression anyway.

On this occasion, I had just been to the local newspaper office to see if I could find anything or anyone interesting enough to put on film. There wasn't too much. Well not too much that hadn't already been done and redone by the old "Town and Around" programme anyway. All I could come up with were a man who had a complete meteorological station set up in his house and a 90-year-old lady who still drove her 1935 Ford to the hairdresser. Nothing out of the ordinary in Taupo, I felt. Until I came out, that is. Then I saw something, just across the road, that had all the makings of a good story.

Right in the centre of town. In the commercial centre, that is, where real estate prices were as high as the weeds in the lake, was an old, unpainted, single-storey wooden house. It was standing on a good quarter-acre of land. Not a conventional insurance office or solicitor's suite, I thought. So, why was it there? Why had it not made way for commercial enterprise. The land alone must have been worth a fortune. I went back in to see the editor.

Apparently the house was occupied by an extremely old Maori lady. So old, that she wore the moko. The genuine thing too, not an indelible ink job. Anyway she wasn't intending moving. Not for all the blandishments in town. It had been her place of residence for years and it would remain so until she died.

The story was good. The house looked great. Now about the lady. I was warned that she was virtually unapproachable. She wouldn't answer the door to callers and was rarely known to speak other than Maori. My best chance, I was told, was to try to catch her whilst she was out in the town shopping. She was sometimes seen shuffling along slowly with the aid of a long staff. But even then there'd be no guarantee that she'd even acknowledge our existence. Pakehas were not her favourite people.

That all sounded really encouraging, I must say. However, there was one other possibility. Apparently a young woman, who was related to her, often came to her home and sat with the old lady. Maybe she could help.

I can't remember how I managed to get it, but I found the woman's address and drove over to see her. She was nursing a young baby when I arrived. I had to hold the mite, whilst the woman dressed to come back with me to the old shack. Yes, this one would be happy to try to introduce me to the lady with the long staff. Perhaps even persuade her to talk to me on film. The lady in question was over 100 years old, I discovered from this new source. I couldn't wait to meet her.

At the back of the house the large section was fenced in at the sides only. The rear part was open. There was a pathway leading up to a verandah, and this is the route my new ally chose to take on her approach. I hovered not too far behind and the camera crew stayed at the end of the overgrown garden. Waiting for a signal.

I'd decided to get this old lady on film. She was almost a national treasure. At best I hoped to be able to talk to her on film, even go inside her home. At worst I would film as much as possible of whatever we glimpsed.

I had to make do with the worst.

The woman with the baby knocked, called and entered. I waited on the verandah. I was taking a chance. Even though she was so old by calendar years, I'd heard she didn't carry the stick just to assist her walking. I could end up with it across my back.

I could hear the two women talking somewhere in the dark interior of the house. My foot and nose were just inside the door. Then movements told me they were coming. I signalled to the crew.

Sure enough, out came the emissary, followed by this amazing old lady. She looked fantastic close up. The skin on her face was parchment thin, drawn tightly over the bones like an expensive leather glove over a clenched fist. I'd seen her before, surely. Maybe on a Goldie painting.

Would she talk to me? The woman I'd brought along would have to act as interpreter. Unfortunately, the conversation was brief. Perhaps one question and no answer to it. Because suddenly the old lady spotted the cameraman and sound recordist walking towards her.

Her reaction was immediate and very voluble. But in Maori. Nevertheless, I pretty well got the message. She obviously didn't want a bar of the microphone for a start. She called it a gun. I tried to explain how innocent our intentions were, but to no avail. In fact I found myself very much on the defensive. No, she didn't resort to the stick wielding, but she threatened all kinds of horrors on our heads. Including calling for the police. So we retreated. As gracefully as possible, of course.

It had been my first rejection since dear Jean Batten had walked out on me, and it wouldn't be my last. This time though, I'd got some film. The cameraman had kept his camera rolling throughout the whole procedure. So we had this formidable old lady with the moko and long staff haranguing both me and the camera. But we didn't use it.

That afternoon, I made contact with one of the old lady's nephews at a sawmill in the district. I wanted to get some information on the recluse and enlist his help in getting some more film of her. The information was sparse and the offer of help unenthusiastic. However, at least I had some scraps to back up, at worst, a wee item, as I said.

In the evening, at my motel, I received a phone call. It was from another nephew. There had been some family discussion and they didn't want the film that we'd already shot used. The old lady was angry. So I gave my promise and left it at that.

Back in Auckland, we had the film processed. It was superb. Only black and white, unfortunately, but her face looked magnificent. Especially when she was mad. I kept my word though, so it was never transmitted. Instead I had to make do with my ninety-year-old lady with the 1935 Ford. She was European, of course.

If it was hard for me to discover a Maori "Character", it was also evident, early on in my career, that I had a lot to learn about the Maori character with a small "c". About the interrelationships of Maoris, particularly in a Pakeha context.

The basic difference between the European and the Maori is the family thing. The Pakeha has wandered further and for longer from his tribe. In most cases, he'll happily slip the knife in under the shoulder blade of his best pal, if it's expedient. Whereas there is still a terribly strong sense of kinship amongst Maoris. It makes it difficult sometimes, I would think, for the zealots and intellectuals who seek to rebel. I know I found it frustrating on one occasion.

At the time there was a big, controversial issue flaring away in the city that was causing considerable heartache amongst certain young Maoris. I don't recall the specific issue, but it had to do with land. Naturally. Anyway, I had the job of bringing two conflicting Maori viewpoints on the subject together in a studio interview. It was guaranteed to be provocative.

One of the men was a very bright young radical who was never far from an issue. He was a favourite of the news media because of his outspoken beliefs and the polish he'd acquired in voicing them. Regularly.

His opponent in this debate was a very respected older Maori. An elder of the tribe whose land was in question. Their previously stated views then were completely opposed. Their lifestyles were totally different. They were both very literate. We were in for a real ding-dong, I supposed.

Not a bit of it. I obviously didn't know anything about the Maori. I hadn't expected them to love and respect each other. I knew nothing of mana.

The young guy would have been spitting fireballs if the man sitting opposite him had been white. Or even, perhaps, if the protagonists had been of the same age. But his anger melted and his argument faltered because of his inbred respect for the older man. It was a washout as a "confrontation", but a delight for me to behold.

I came into contact with something of a similar quality again sometime later. I was filming a special ceremony on a very small marae in a remote part of Northland. The surrounding area had previously been all but abandoned. The local Maoris had moved away to seek work in the towns. The meeting house and the cookhouse had become unused and derelict. It had been deserted.

Then someone decided it shouldn't be left to die and fade away. A Pakeha organisation from Auckland, interested in preserving New Zealand's heritage, got together with the few remaining Maoris in the district. Between them, they decided to rebuild everything.

Every weekend or spare holiday, the Aucklanders went up to work on the project, until it was completed. Then the local tribe reconsecrated and rededicated the reborn marae. It was one of the most moving experiences I'd ever witnessed.

Tribes came from all over the country. From parts of both islands. They travelled for days by boat, by train, by bus. To be there together.

On the day, huddled in blankets to keep out the crisp, dawn air, old and young waited their turn outside the marae. Each tribe entered the confines of the sacred ground according to an order of precedence they all seemed to know instinctively. Then they greeted each other. Rekindling something in each one that was put there a million years ago.

I was just a bystander. However, I couldn't help but share in the incredibly strong feeling of family unity that simply flooded the whole scene. That special atmosphere can't be recreated in the monster booze barns in the city suburbs. But that, unhappily, is the other, overweighted side of the scales.

The longer I stayed in Auckland, the more disenchanted I became with pursuing and recording the heavy social issues. The city seemed to abound in them at one time. Or maybe they're always there and they just got aired more and more often. The plight of the unwed mother, the plight of the Symphonia, the plight of the suburban housewife, the plight of the overweight, the plight of boat owners because of the shortage of marina berths, the plight of the old, the plight of the young. I did them all. Not to mention the plight of the dairy farmers in the Waikato, the plight of the miners in Huntly and the plight of having to live in Hamilton.

However, it wasn't just the constant tone of despair that the subject matter brought with it, it was also the way it had to be treated. There was just no opportunity for good old-fashioned bias. You were always expected to be fair. Give all sides to the argument and make no personal comment.

That took a bit of doing sometimes, I can tell you. Especially when, as a father of six children, I had to listen to someone rabbiting on about birth control. Telling the viewer of the horrors of overpopulation and the irresponsibility of people who have more than one and a half children. Particularly if I knew that the person talking kept two Great Danes and a Persian cat as pets and fed them on steak and chips.

Quite often some of these crusaders would almost make me gag at their pompous self-righteousness. But good old TV always allowed them to use its services as their soap box. Allowing equal time for an opposite "expert" view to be put, of course.

In election year, the NZBC management was so worried and oversensitive about this equal time nonsense that the situation could become ludicrous.

Say, for instance, a woman appeared in a programme, pointed to her little child's dirty bare feet and said: "I just can't afford to buy him shoes, the price has gone up so much recently." My gosh. The next day the phone would run hot.

"Who allowed that woman to make that statement unchallenged? There have been enquiries from the minister. We'll have to interview a government member tonight to put the matter straight."

So that night, pure and smiling under the hot lights, the under-secretary in charge of shoe prices would be patronising us. He'd explain first how external influences beyond the government's control had caused the price of shoe leather to increase. Then he'd drop the paternal smile and the dirt would come out.

His departmental officers had checked on the woman who'd made the remark and discovered that she wasn't simply an innocent victim of inflation. No. She was a well-known troublemaker and questionable mother, who had had *de facto* relationships with at least three gas fitters from Taranaki. Not only that, she couldn't be so hard up, he would claim, since she'd been seen buying the boy an ice cream only the day before she appeared on television.

Now the field was wide open. Equal time, remember. So next we'd have an opposition spokesman on shoe leather.

He'd front up with a sheath of notes hanging out of his wee plastic brief case, looking even smugger than his predecessor. His answers, despite the fact that he had the latest "stastistics", would be completely predictable. The woman's plight had nothing to do with the previous administration. Let's get that quite clear. Next, if the government had taken his party's advice thirty years earlier, external pressures would never have affected the nation's feet.

At the same time, myriads of women's rights organisations would have been demanding time and the opportunity to defend the poor woman. They wouldn't be so worried about the lack of shoes, but they'd defend to the death the woman's right to share her favours or her ice cream with whomsoever she pleased. And so it would go on and on. I dreaded election year.

Besides, I was really having a lot of doubt about the effectiveness of earnest reporting altogether. For me anyway.

Oh, I don't for one minute deny that there is a real need for strenuous, thorough investigation and presentation of the issues in society. That of course is every communication medium's responsibility. I also think that perhaps some people can afford to take themselves seriously while they do it. They have either the face or the voice for the job. But I don't think I ever really did.

There was another reason too. As a person who was interested in making my living from television, I had to be a realist also. One fact that was beginning to dawn on me was that lighter subject treatment seemed to get greater audience response. This fact was graphically illustrated to me when two vastly different pieces of my work were transmitted during the same week. To basically the same audience. The first one was a heavy. It was a mini-documentary on a very real and serious problem existing in Auckland. Malnutrition. Especially amongst Polynesian infants.

For this, I spent a lot of time researching and then filming frighteningly debilitated babies and talking to paediatricians and health department officials. I visited homes with Plunket nurses and witnessed scenes I could hardly believe. It was a blight on man's conscience and made a sad and emotional film. It should have shocked. I practically choked on my own commentary which I read live as the programme was transmitted.

The second item was about a little arbour that the Auckland City Council had created on the site of a recently demolished old shop building. The space it took up was very small, only about twenty-five feet by ten feet. In this area, the council had first laid a pretty cobblestone flooring. At the back, abutting a rough stone wall six feet high, were some low troughs of earth, waiting for plants. And in front of those were two wooden bench seats. There were also more flower bed troughs in the front, between the seats and the public footpath. The little wall at the rear, by the way, separated this bijou garden from the yard of a greengrocer's shop. His outside toilet, which sounded like Niagara in a storm, was adjacent.

Now, this little retreat was set in an extremely scruffy part of town. About two blocks away from the main shopping streets. In my opinion, if any planner had had any real desire to bring beauty to the surrounding drabness, he should have insisted that the whole area be razed.

As it was, the setting was the most incongruous thing one could imagine. The council said it was designed to provide a much-needed place for office workers to sit and eat their lunch in. (More than six at a time would have crowded the space.) The sentiments were laudable. But the practicability and the aesthetics were ludicrous.

The pavement all around it was broken up and in need of repair. The air was deep blue from diesel and petrol fumes spewed out by passing cars and trucks, great numbers of trucks, because this ill-conceived oasis was placed at the corner of an extremely busy intersection. One road carried all the heavy transport trucks on a steep incline down or up from the wharves. As you can imagine, when those articulated monsters geared their way past the spot, not only was it dangerous to continue trying to breathe, but anyone sitting there would be deafened.

I made a tiny film. I simply used humour to illustrate a few of the points I've mentioned. As the reporter, I represented the "little man" who takes up the council's invitation to tarry a while and eat his lunch. The camera and tape recorder did the rest. They merely had to faithfully record the scene: the pollution, the din and the absurdity.

When I got up from a seat and left, having choked on my fume-flavoured lunch, I "accidentally" tripped over the broken asphalt pavement. Then I limped off.

The project had no doubt cost the ratepayers thousands. As a viewer, he was very interested. The reaction was fantastic. People phoned, people wrote. Newspapers wanted to do follow-up stories and take pictures of me back at the scene. It was astonishing.

The next day, the council even sent men to the scene to repair the footpath. And the item was only two and a half minutes long.

On the other hand, not a single soul had commented on the film about the suffering babies. No newspaper critic had written a word. Not a phone had rung. It was very revealing. From then on I decided that I would strive to inject as much humour and lightness of tone into my work as possible.

Not that it always comes off, mind you. A light-hearted *exposé* of the exorbitant prices at the Easter Show almost brought grief. To me, that is.

I'd visited the show with three of my children and a camera crew. The object was to film our actions and reactions whilst out to enjoy a day at the fair. The point the little film made, quite innocently, was that it was a very expensive exercise indeed for a family.

The camera showed me paying the much-too-high entrance fee, and turning from a carefree, fun-loving dad to a mid-winter Scrooge of necessity. I refused to pay for any rides, however much the children begged. The camera showed the faces and the prices. I turned down a visit to the Ghost House. I even refused the chance to watch one-legged dwarfs wrestling with alligators. Instead I dragged the poor little dears back and forth through the tediously boring manufacturers' display stands. Finally though, when all three were visibly fed up, I decided to splurge.

Just inside the entrance gate, and on our leaden-footed way out, I stopped at the hot air balloon concession. The price made me blanch, but I was committed. I bought one for my smallest child, a button of a thing with long curly hair and a very expressive face. She was about six at the time. Anyway I paid the 50 cents or more and gave her the string. For the first time that afternoon, the camera could capture some joy. But the glimpse was fleeting. So too was the balloon. Within seconds, the child's face was doom and the balloon was airborne, making fairly fast time towards Karangahape Road to the north.

It was a good ending, assisted by a remark from me which, try as I may, I can't recall. However I would swear on a pack of All Blacks that no malice was intended.

You can imagine my surprise then, when the gentleman who owned the balloon concession turned up the next day at Broadcasting House demanding to see me. The receptionist phoned me to let me know that a very angry gentleman was in the foyer asking for me. She suggested, quite calmly, that he probably intended to tear me limb from limb.

It's at such times that there is something to be said for being part of a team. The editor of the programme was always responsible for its contents. So, at my request, the call was transferred to him. Fortunately he was a rather big chap, physically, and the matter was dealt with fairly swiftly without blood or tears being spilt.

But it illustrates just how easy it is for someone to gather a completely wrong impression from something that was intended entirely innocently.

I remember another little skit I was involved in that wasn't quite received in the way it was intended to be. This one was a "send-up" of "professional protesters". It was for the same news magazine programme that ran every evening in Auckland, "This Day". Another regular on the programme, Rhys]ones, and I had worked up an idea based on something a politician had claimed.

I'm not sure whether or not it was "you know who" or some lesser mortal in the National Party, but whoever it was, he was deadly serious. The charge was that the same demonstrators had been seen at protest actions in different parts of the country and for widely differing causes. These people were obviously being hired, was the man's brilliant deduction. And the "boys in blue" apparently had irrefutable evidence in their little box brownies.

So we decided to do a spoof on the contention.

First we shot some film of students working in a "secret factory" making banners and training for various "causes". While they worked at their benches or did press-ups in the aisles, they were "interviewed". Shamelessly, they all admitted that they were in fact full-time demonstrators who could be hired for money. A sort of Rent-a-crowd. The "secret" factory, incidentally, was the design department of Northern Television.

Then we had a "live" studio set up. With someone that Rhys had managed to track down for an exclusive interview on the subject. This mystery guest turned out to be the President of the Professional Demonstrators Union. It was in fact me, with a long tangled wig, a straggly beard, army battledress, beads and sandals. The conventional union leader's dress.

The interview was done tongue-in-cheek, and that's not easy when you're chewing gum at the same time, believe me.

Nevertheless, the atmosphere was electric as the full scope of this element in society was revealed. A major point that was discussed was the demand from the demonstrators for higher rates for increased risks. This was several years before the Accident Compensation Act was introduced, don't forget.

One of the risks, or occupational hazards, that "the members" sought some relief for was their piles. Their haemorrhoids. Brought on by constantly having to sit down on wet roadways to obstruct law and order.

The union leader insisted on both the necessity and relevance of professional demonstrators. He called on the old to take more active interest and participation.

We thought it was a bit of a laugh. Nothing more. But the public didn't. The following week, I received a letter from a viewer enclosing a cutting from the *Northern Advocate*. It was the Whangarei paper's editorial; totally occupied with the subject of professional demonstrators. The article was headed "Payment of Protesters", and contained no fewer than fourteen paragraphs on the subject, using as its hook the television item. Here are two of the paragraphs:

> "Who could have failed to register concern at the frank admission of a fascinatingly or frighteningly (how you see it) bewhiskered young gentleman that some protesters, by receiving payment and going out 'on assignment', were straight-out professionals?"

The final paragraph summed up the writer's responsible editorial opinion on the subject:

> "In fact, payment of protesters likens itself alarmingly to payment of mobs, with anarchy only a scream away."

Well, we didn't scream exactly, but we did have a good hoot. It was almost as amusing as the letter on the same topic that was printed in all seriousness in the *Waikato Times*. Here is paragraph two of that missile which was written by one, Trevor Betts of Cambridge:

"This individual (the president of the protesters union) had the audacity to pledge his whole-hearted support for any budding demonstrators while he haughtily faced the TV camera chewing gum, hair in a dishevelled mess and with his work jacket button undone. You could see his contempt for society just oozing out."

And I had thought I'd become a well-known member of that programme's reporting team. Maybe it was time for me to move on. Even out of disguise, my credibility was beginning to fade. I was getting a completely unwarranted reputation for sending up people and places. Rubbish of course.

I may not have taken them as seriously as some would have liked, but I would never have "sent them up". Even the Frontiersmen. That magnificently uniformed band of men who train and pledge to defend our shores and in the meantime patrol our car parks. Boy scout hats, silver epaulets, jodhpurs and all. Or the incredible Western club in Glen Eden.

Just another men's club, I was told by one of the members as he hitched his station wagon outside the double-fronted shop premises and bow-legged his way inside. He was dressed in full cowboy gear, and so too were another twenty or thirty men in the "club". All wore six-shooters in their holsters.

The shops that served as an arena for their fantasies were rented. However these would-be habitues of the wild west must have obtained a long lease, for they had a bar set up in one corner. And not only that. Through a pair of swing doors they had a shooting range. In fact the whole décor was created to be as authentic as possible. When they weren't shoved up to the bar, or slinging the lead through the doors, they'd be round the table with the cards. But throughout the evening, seemingly for no apparent reason, a couple of them would get up together and call for a draw. Over to the corner they'd go, slowly, like John Wayne and Gary Cooper, then they'd face each other, eyes like ice. A signal, and down their hands would flash. John Wayne would win by a click Nobody actually fired any powder, thank God.

This was their hobby, of course. Bankers, motor mechanics, insurance clerks, all kinds. And they were totally immersed in it, spurs and all. Now who would be rude enough to "send up" that? I just didn't treat it too seriously, that's all.

The only person I ever intentionally "sent up", in fact, was a gentleman by the name of Alan Whicker. And he loved it. But it wasn't easy, believe me.

The assignment wasn't my idea, for one thing. It was the brainchild of the programme editor. "Hayes over Whicker" was the concept. Unhappily it was based on the mistaken belief that Mr Whicker and I had something in common. That's a polite way of summing up a very big misapprehension on the part of some of New Zealand's so-called television critics.

You see, many of them over the years have compared my style with his, or Johnny Morris's, or anyone else they could think of that would save them some trouble. It's much easier, if you've only got four column inches for a programme review, to use a visual analogy that everyone will recognise. Easier, that is, than trying to describe someone's way of working in your own words. So in their innocent but clumsy way, some of these writers on television foisted on to the public the idea that I had modelled my style and even my voice on Alan Whicker. Actually, the comparison with Johnny Morris came later.

(In the same way, when I was a radio announcer in the 'sixties, my voice was reckoned to be like David Frost's. Only I'd never even heard the guy.)

The clue is of course that basically we all have fairly common English accents. Slightly nasal. You'll find even more in England. It's got something to do with the dampness I believe.

My main aim throughout my time in television, was to experiment with as many styles and forms as possible. For one purpose: to communicate to the viewer. In other words, I tried to be original. I endeavoured, always, to work from myself and mould my material in the way I thought would best communicate its content and feeling. That's why the little film item I did when Alan Whicker was the subject intentionally adopted his own style. And I was prepared to lampoon myself in the process.

The British documentary maker was planning to make a series of programmes about New Zealand. We knew he was arriving on an early flight from Fiji.

We started with the arrival. Air New Zealand was flying him in on a "contra deal". That means the tickets were gratis, in exchange for a shot of the plane here and there in the films. It's become the greatest *cliché* in the business.

Anyway, before he landed we shot some film of me arriving at the airport and getting out of an old car. A very battered 1954 Standard Vanguard. As I stepped from the car, we froze the picture and later superimposed my name. That was to inter-cut with a shot of Whicker stepping out, in his usual style, from the doorway of an international jet.

So we had to get the cameraman on to the tarmac. The restricted area. Not too difficult a task when the film will include a shot of the local airline's plane. It had all been jacked up before by Air New Zealand's public relations man. No sweat.

In the meantime, with that man's assurance that I'd get the first bite of the apple, I'd laid my plans. I'd arranged with the management of the airport restaurant to do the interview there. The idea was to use a typical Whicker setting: around the breakfast table. The manager was even happy to supply a waitress and whatever food we required for props. So we had pre-set the lights for the filming.

Next, we took a shot of me walking through the airport concourse. This would match a shot we intended taking of Alan Whicker walking from the plane to customs. After that, in continuity I hoped to get some film of both of us meeting and walking together to the restaurant. But first the shot of the Air New Zealand plane landing, and Whicker at the top of the stairs.

Well, he came in on a BOAC flight. That was blunder number one from the P.R. man. My cameraman was on his toes, thank goodness, and got the shot at the door as planned.

Next, I had to arrange to meet the man himself. I spoke to his producer, Fred Burnley, who'd already been in the country for a couple of weeks. He was now waiting to greet Whicker himself.

Burnley was less than optimistic. Alan doesn't like interviews at all. I shouldn't bank on it, but he'd try to persuade him. The most I could expect would be a couple of minutes. I needed at least half an hour. While all this was going on and my crew and I were hovering as close to the customs benches as we legally could, a crowd was gathering behind us. Not a mass of the general public, no. A mass of interested parties. Dozens of them. Reporters from newspapers, reporters from magazines, teams of public relations bodies from Air New Zealand and BOAC, squads of others from the Department of Internal Affairs, even more from the Tourist and Publicity Department. Only the Department of Maori Affairs was without representation, I'm certain.

It was beginning to look like a circus, there were so many people. I sought out the P.R. man once again. He was supposed to be organising everything. I needed his reassurance that I would be able to do my interview first. In fact I wanted to do two set-ups. One for a brief piece for network news and a longer, more leisurely chat for our magazine programme. Both films were intended for the same evening's screening. That meant we would have to rush them back to the television channel for processing and editing.

The man in the pale blue Air New Zealand jacket gave me his word. All the other reporters would wait outside the restaurant in a small lounge until I'd finished with Whicker. Fine. Now, all I had to know was if the subject was going to co-operate or not. I took a chance. I told the cameraman just to run the camera and follow me.

Alan Whicker was just through customs and talking to his producer and another chap as I approached. I held out my hand. I was in luck. He took it and we met with a handshake on camera. I chatted to him and led him away towards the restaurant stairway:

"Would you like some breakfast?"

"Well, what I'd really like is a pee", he answered. "Is there a place round here you can get one of those?" And that's how it started.

When he was ready and comfortable, he came up to the restaurant for the filming. And so, would you believe it, did the entire mass of people who had turned up for his arrival. My Air New Zealand man had either been overwhelmed or he had a warped sense of humour. The result was that instead of a cosy *tête-à-tête* with the maestro on his own, we were required to be two performing seals for an audience. Some of them sat looking at us from less than three feet away. It's a wonder they didn't applaud any of his answers to my questions.

I couldn't even move them between film rolls. It took a few minutes to rethread new film and sound tape before we could continue. However when I asked them if they'd like to use that time to ask their questions, they sat like mummies, transfixed.

The only consolation about the whole experience was Whicker's courtesy and patience. Particularly since I knew he'd been completely turned off by the boorishness of these tactless intruders. He showed it, though, only when he was leaving. He walked past them without stopping.

So instead of filing news stories about the arrival of this distinguished journalist to our shores, the reporters present wrote critiques about our performances. For instance, how I had become angry at interruptions from loudspeaker announcements. We'd had to stop a couple of times for flight arrivals and departures to be proclaimed throughout the building.

One newspaper column that appeared the following

morning even quoted, or rather misquoted, part of a private conversation I had with Whicker before the camera was running. So I was public domain! It was a bit of a farce. So much for the "send up".

Near the end of 1973, I moved my family and my allegiances south. However, I was to return many times in the following years to shoot film.

CHAPTER FOUR

Back on the Mainland

IN 1979 I WATCHED a British-made documentary which showed the lifestyle of a young woman who'd been born without arms. She'd been a victim of the thalidomide tragedy.
What the film showed however, was a happy, well-adjusted young woman who was married and the mother of two children. One of which she was nursing.
On the screen, she seemed completely self-confident and happy. Her domestic life was as routine as any other housewife's. Except that she did all her chores with her feet. She seemed to have no difficulty at all preparing vegetables and cooking them. The lady just hoisted herself up onto the kitchen counter top and did with her feet what she would otherwise have done with her hands.
After watching this lass operating in this way for a short while you almost forgot she was lacking two limbs. The two that most of us rely on so much, at that. Especially when she sat on the floor, changed the baby's nappy and cradled the infant in her legs whilst she fed it its bottle.
The interviewer in the programme was as awestruck at her dexterity as many viewers would no doubt have been. However the girl explained that she was merely behaving naturally. Instinctively. She didn't miss having arms, she'd never had them. As far as she was concerned, she was complete. Her real self was in no way deformed, or handicapped.
She'd been lucky though in her choice of parents. Judging by what she said and what they said, when we saw them, their attitude had been healthy and loving from the start.
The film took me back to the young boy that I filmed, several years earlier, in Christchurch, Steven Roome.

Stevie was the fifth child born to Alex and Joyce Roome. Their first four children were girls. They'd waited fourteen years for their son to arrive. He came into the world without arms.

But Stevie was different again. His physical condition was not caused by the drug Thalidomide. It was something of a mystery in fact. The mother had been sick during pregnancy and had taken medication. But nothing that even hinted at possible danger, and there'd been no record kept. His birth then was considered a rare fluke. They were told it was something that might happen only once in a million births.

The boy was seven when I met him. He'd obviously been succoured on love. His bright blue eyes shone with confidence. His enthusiasm for living was as exciting as any healthy seven year old's should be and probably more than most are. Already, this wiry, blond-mopped youngster had lived through more adventures than many people do in a lifetime.

When he was one year old, he'd been off to Australia to meet another boy who'd also been born armless. The Australian boy was a few years his senior and the Roomes were anxious to discover how others coped with circumstances similar to their own. In New Zealand there was nowhere to go to compare notes. Stevie was unique but not alone, as the family was to discover when the young Kiwi was three. Because then he became the target for a lot of love from a lot of people throughout New Zealand.

You see, it was at that time that Stevie and his mum were planning to go to Britain. His father, after paying off the cost of the trip to Aussie, had set his mind on it.

Both Alex and Joyce Roome had one philosophy as far as their son was concerned. That he should benefit from the experience of others and the very best and latest advice that medical science could provide. Wherever it could be obtained. That meant sacrifice. For the father, a fitter and turner by trade, it meant working all hours possible to raise as much money as possible. For all of them it meant scrimping and saving.

Their aim was to educate themselves completely to adjust to and deal with this unexpected twist in their lives. To do, and obtain, whatever was necessary to help the boy live a normal and happy life. In Europe, new developments were taking place all the time in the field of rehabilitative medicine. By whatever means it took, they'd decided, the boy would go there to benefit from them. The sad reality too was that there were many many people in that part of the world whose experience Stevie and his mother could learn from.

Then their story got out. To the neighbours first. Soon it spread to residents of Waltham, Beckenham and Sydenham, three of the more humble suburbs of the city of Christchurch. The response wasn't so humble though. They set up an appeal in a local grocery store, to send the mother and child to Britain.

The owner of the store, who was one of the main instigators of the move, put it this way: "This is an opportunity everyone has been waiting for. We've always wanted to do something to help Steven and this is it."

It certainly was. The money rolled in. From pensioners, from the youth of the district, from other parents and from wee children. The local schools joined in too, holding their own appeals. That's when a Christchurch paper printed the story. Then the balloon went up.

New Zealanders aren't renowned for showing their feelings. They play things fairly close to the chest. On the face of it anyway. But when there's a need, just watch them go.

The donations came in from everywhere. From Invercargill in the south to Auckland in the north. Indeed Radio I, then one of the only two private radio stations in the country, set up their own appeal. More than that, they offered to pay the return air fares for the proposed trip.

However, Alex Roome was a proud man. He'd worked and saved for this project himself. Besides, he wanted his wife to have a holiday first. So he insisted on paying for her and his son to travel to Britain by sea. The radio station then could bring them back.

By the time they were due to leave, almost $5,000 had been raised. It was an expression that touched the family very deeply. Their venture was assured and a small trust fund for the boy established. Six months later, the boy returned with a lot of knowledge and a new pair of artificial arms.

In 1974, I got in touch with the family and asked if I might make a film about Steven. He was just about to have a birthday. The family agreed, provided I could function around their work hours. Now both parents were flat out earning as much as they could. Not just for future trips overseas, but for all the new equipment and alterations required in the home to accommodate the lad as he grew up.

It was an easy film to make, as it turned out. Stevie's spirit was contagious. His maturity was real and confident without a trace of precocity. And I liked his mum and dad, anyway. Well I had good reason to, I discovered. Alex Roome, who was about the same age as me, had actually come from London. In fact, he'd lived about a mile away from where I spent a good few years of my life. In England, he'd been mechanic to New Zealand speedway ace, Ronnie Moore. Now they were neighbours in Christchurch.

At this time, young Stevie had two passions. One was speedway at Templeton, the other was soccer. One he watched. The other, he definitely played. We even filmed him scoring a goal in a club match at Hagley Park. We filmed him riding a bike too. He had absolutely no fear, he just laid his chest across the handlebars for steering and pedalled like fury. I wouldn't be in the least bit surprised if he doesn't do the same thing with a motorbike one day.

He could swim too. We filmed him in a pool, as one newspaper critic later described it: "swimming like a little human minnow". However, that little minnow even dived in head first.

The boy had the perfect temperament for filming. Whatever we asked him to do, he did it willingly and usually with a smile. Working with his arms on in the classroom, walking along home with his mate from school. Sitting on the dining room table ferociously playing the "war game" with his father. Sitting in front of the television set eating his dinner - with his fork held in his toes. His patience was incredible.

Filming, particularly interiors of houses, can be excruciatingly tedious. The right mood has to be established. The correct lighting has to be achieved. Anybody not intended to be in the shot ·has to be quiet and keep clear. It can be very wearing, and at times can create tensions. Not for Stevie though. He took it all in his stride. Then, when he sat down on the bathroom floor and demonstrated how he cleaned his teeth, he all but broke my heart.

First, standing on one leg like a graceful flamingo, he got his toothbrush and then the toothpaste down from the sink top, with his other foot. Then he sat down, undid the paste top with his toes and placed the brush on the floor beside him. Holding the tube between his toes, he then squeezed a small worm of white paste onto the bristles of the brush. Then he put the cap back on the tube, picked up the brush and brushed his teeth. When he had given them a thorough going over, he stood up and rinsed out over the sink.

The whole operation took some time. Every move was made with total concentration.

He certainly was an unusual boy. Indeed, we all thought he was special. The cameraman, Hamdani Milas, who had joined me in Christchurch, was so touched that he wrote a piece of music for him. I used it throughout the film as "Stevie's theme". I called the programme "One in a Million" and the title had nothing to do with his physically rare birth, believe me.

The twenty minute documentary proved quite a success. It was shown at a none-too-popular time. Six o'clock on a Sunday evening. Programming has never been a strong point of New Zealand broadcasting. However, outside of sports programmes, viewers rated it the top local programme for 1974. I was pleased with it for another reason though.

Not long after it was shown throughout New Zealand, some

very relevant and necessary legislation was passed by parliament. A bill requiring that doctors register the births of so-called "deformed" babies was pushed through. It had been pending for some time. So Stevie had made his point.

There are two sections of New Zealand society that I suppose are more maligned than most. One of them is the watersiders and the other, the people who manage and operate the railways. Or as some say, mismanage and operate them. Anyway, both seem constantly to be subjected to criticism, abuse and worse, and both of them are essential to the economic wellbeing of New Zealand and its people.

In a way, what goes on and comes off at our wharves and how efficiently our railways handle things vitally affects everyone. These two key industries can cause us to enjoy great comfort or they can make life very difficult. Many accuse them of being politically obstreperous because of the power over us they possess. Unfortunately, neither of them enjoys a reputation for great diligence and industriousness. In that respect, history is no friend to either. Over the years they've become the butt of the comedian.

Perhaps the worst aspersions are cast against the wharfie, with innocent little jokes like this one: there were these two watersiders, see, walking along one of the wharves at Lyttelton, talking. When suddenly one of them broke off from the conversation, turned and slammed his foot down on a small snail just behind him, crushing it.

"What's the matter with you, Bert?" said the other man, "What did you do that for so viciously?"

Bert scraped the sole of his shoe on the ground carefully and replied: "I was fed up with the damn thing, it's been following me around all day!"

That nasty story was told to me by a railwayman by the way. Ironical, because for sheer cussedness, in my experience anyway, some of the gentlemen of New Zealand Rail take some beating.

I don't recommend it, but if you want to test out my

assertion, try a trip on the Southerner. The pride of the South Island railtrack.

You'll have to be in a position to waste two full days of your life to do the experiment. That is, make a journey by rail from Christchurch to Invercargill and, if you've got the stamina, back again.

It's my sincere belief that not too many make the return trip. Not because they don't wish to get back again, no. It's simply because they can't face the prospect of repeating the ordeal they suffered on the outward leg. Indeed, I would go so far as to suggest that the city of Invercargill is settled by people who originally bought return tickets on the Southerner and who have been reluctant to take up the option on the second part.

The journey, officially (if you can really apply that term to that particular branch of the public service) takes around ten hours. Ten monotonous, tedious hours of starting and stopping. Through scenery that is so similar for vast stretches that it might as well be a painting on the window.

Whoever decided the route for the rail must never have raised his eyes above his knees whilst he surveyed. My gosh there's a lot of grass in the South Island. The heart nearly stops with excitement when you catch the occasional glimpse of the sea or even a farm building.

It was my own fault, of course. It's a weakness of mine to try to experience new things. I'd never been on a long distance train journey in New Zealand and I had to do it once at least. I had to go to Invercargill to do some research. I could have flown. I believe there was still a daily flight. Or I could have driven. But, no, this time I'd take the Southerner and really see the countryside. I assumed I'd also be able to get some reading done. I should have known better.

Train drivers the world over have one thing in common. They know by some strange instinct how to vary the speed of their locomotives to cause the greatest annoyance to their passengers. If, by chance there is anything vaguely interesting to be seen through the windows, the train practically leaves the rails with its pace. On the other hand, whenever you are satiated with the flow of passing sights and return to your book, the velocity changes dramatically. Then the thing moves with rhythmic deliberateness. It sits full weighted on the tracks, like an elephant astride a pencil, feeling out every sleeper join that it passes ponderously over. Slowly the words in your hands become hazier and hazier until, finally, you give up and doze off into oblivion. But never for very long.

Inevitably, just as your chin hits your chest, the train groans to a halt at a station and you are assailed by the sounds of warfare. Screams from relatives greeting relatives. Explosions from doors slammed vehemently as people come grunting and shouting aboard. Shrill whistleblowing as the stationmaster remembers what he's there for, and wailing from the baby who's just joined your coach. Bleary eyed and cheated, you try to return to your dream. That's when the train hostess assaults you.

On a train the simple yet appetising phrase: "Lunch is now being served" becomes a threat. Ignore it and you'll be glared to death. Obey it and you'll discover that the driver can make the carriages go sideways as well as forwards.

On the Southerner, you sit up at a counter for refreshment. Instant refreshment. Instant coffee, instant tea, instant orange. But if you want anything else you'll have to wait a minute. The food is sitting staring at you above the counter in plastic windowed shelves. You wonder how many return trips the sandwiches and salads opposite have already made. Too many, you decide. You settle for instant tea. In your cup, in your saucer, on your sleeve and down your chin. Then you rhumba your way back to your seat. To read the advertisements above the luggage rack, again and again and again. And so it goes on.

Finally, limp and mal-shaped from sitting, you arrive red-eyed and exhausted in Invercargill. That's if you're lucky. Believe me, the journey can go a lot less smoothly. My return trip did. Despite my precautions.

Once I had recovered from the ride down and done my business I found an excuse to travel up to Dunedin to meet someone before returning home. My visit to the "Edinburgh of the South" wasn't entirely necessary for my work, but I deemed it essential for my overall wellbeing. I decided to rent a car and drive there, stay overnight and thus cut two hours off the train ride back to Christchurch. My plan was good. However, the Railways Department must have got wind of it. I wasn't allowed to get away as easily as that.

For those of you who have yet to enjoy the pleasure of a Southerner odyssey, I must explain one small detail. There is a single track for the whole distance. The idea being that the minimum of land would be appropriated from the thousands of acres of grass over which it travels. But there are in fact, two places where the Railways Department broadened its vision; where two stretches of track exist side by side. These dashes of sophistication occur at a spot called Goodwood and again seven miles further up the line at Palmerston. Both roughly midway between the two termini. It's at one or other of these rural delights that the train crews change over. The up train people switch with the down train people. In that way neither team has to endure the entire journey, one way. The switchover is normally done fairly smoothly I believe. Each crew having powdered their noses in readiness a good half-hour before it takes place.

Unfortunately, on my deviously planned abbreviated trip, something went wrong. I sensed it as we slowed and crawled funereally through Goodwood. I knew it when we arrived, eventually, at Palmerston. The other train didn't show up. Not for ages anyway.

This extra little trial occurred about an hour after the gentle threat that "lunch is being served". I had decided to risk the glares on this occasion. I'd had something in Dunedin and could last out until afternoon tea, I felt. Then came the hiatus.

Now Palmerston is not the most exciting place in the world at the best of times. I don't think it professes to be. It was named after a former British Prime Minister, Lord

Palmerston, who apparently wasn't the most distinguished chap to fill that post. Indeed, it has been written of him that: "there is no enduring achievement to his credit, but he left many bitter legacies." One of them I suggest is to site the Southerner train junction at the place that bears his name.

It is farming country, the day was warm and somebody had been fertilising. Not the best location to be stranded on a stationary train, I can assure you.

The crew agreed. Well most of them did. They got off the train and went for a walk into town. Those who remained sat in the refreshment room or lounged around the doorways. No one said a word to the passengers.

Why were we waiting? All of us in the coach were beginning to wonder. So after about twenty minutes, I decided to find out. I went to the refreshment room. Officially, it should still have been open. According to the times printed on the menu, that is. I asked a couple of the hostesses what the problem was. Neither knew. I asked for a coffee, I was refused. No one could be served whilst the train was changing crews, I was told. The refreshment bar was closed. It didn't matter a tinker's cuss that the other train wasn't even in sight or that the waiters had nothing else to do.

"You'll have to wait 'til the new crew gets on."

"Where are they?" I asked, just for the hell of it.

"Wouldn't have a clue, mate."

By now, the crew members who'd gone for a walk had returned and were sitting on the edge of the platform opposite eating fish and chips, with their legs dangling over the side.

That's an idea, I thought, as I started to open the door. "You can't leave the train." That was an order too. My informant had enough gold braid on his uniform and hat to be an admiral. "No one must leave the train, sir. That's regulations."

"Well, what about them," I pointed to the group on the platform who were by then emptying down cans of soft drinks.

"Well," said the admiral, "they are changing trains. They're waiting to board the down train."

"Where is it?"

"Well, we don't know, it should be here. It must be held up."

There is a limit, of course, as to how far you can pursue a subject in those conditions before it becomes farcical. I knew that for every question I asked, there would be an official answer. There has to be, even if it makes no sense.

I retreated to my seat. About an hour later, I again went to find out.

This time, I was in luck. Somebody actually knew something. Presumably, when the fish and chips were all eaten and the soft drink all drunk, someone had acted. One of the crew had been interested enough to phone ahead. The answer was slowly relayed back: "They're working on the line a few miles up the track." Now at last we knew. Although we still didn't know how long "they'd" be. Indeed the passengers were never officially told of either piece of information.

Eventually, then, the down train slid alongside. We'd been delayed the best part of two hours. I had gained absolutely nothing by stopping over at Dunedin. I was destined to be on the Southerner for the full ten hours whatever I did. And whether it was going or not.

Now I was feeling peckish too. So, after allowing about ten minutes for the train to get underway and for the crew to re-open the refreshment bar, I went along for a cup of tea. I thought I might even throw caution to the winds and try one of their cakes. That's what I thought anyway.

By now, it was the official tea-serving period. We had not as yet been officially harangued with the news, it's true. Nevertheless, quite a few had already made their way to the cafeteria coach. There were very few vacant stools left to sit at when I arrived.

I found one and sat down. Immediately, I became aware of the other people's eyes on me. Some of the busy conversation had stopped. A youngish guy with his gold braided tunic and his dirt stained collar unbuttoned approached me from the other side of the bar. "We're closed, we're not serving yet."

"What do you mean," I retorted, stunned at his news. "What are all these people doing then?" There were cups of instant tea and plates of instant sandwiches everywhere.

"They're the crew, they haven't had their lunch yet. Did you have your lunch?" He was a confident young man. I suppose that's why he'd unbuttoned his collar and jacket with such irreverent abandon.

"Well, no, I didn't want anything then, but..."

"Oh, well, you should have had lunch. We're not serving now." He was quite adamant. The others each side of me were nodding in agreement too.

I was getting a little angry at the situation. "But this is the official tea time!" I mustered all the authority I could for that line. It made not one iota of an impression.

"Yes," he agreed, "but we won't be serving tea for..." he looked at his watch, then at the clock on the wall, "for another, oh, say, three-quarters of an hour. Sorry." And he went off to pour a colleague a cup of tea. The rest of the conversation picked up again and I was left standing there watching the crew eating their late lunch.

So much for the Southerner. I don't think I'll bother to travel that way again. Not unless I get a job with the New Zealand Railways that is.

There's one fascinating place in the South Island that the Southerner doesn't stop at. It's the tiny borough of Naseby, on the Maniototo plains of Central Otago. The smallest borough in New Zealand and probably the smallest in the world. It had a population of 109 when I was last there. And I met most of them, I do believe.

Anyway the reasons why the main trunk route from Christchurch to Invercargill doesn't touch this spot are twofold. Firstly there's no fish and chip shop there. Secondly the Kakanui mountains are. Naseby actually sits on the hem of the range and is itself some 2000 feet above sea level. Or as the town sign-writer prefers, above worry level.

Certainly the cemetery is. It's well signposted too. Right at the beginning of the main street. The sign points up a rising lane, along with the ubiquitous AA warning that there is "no exit". I thought that was a wee bit unnecessary.

I was in Naseby to make a film about the community as it prepared for the local body elections. I thought it might make an interesting contrast to the ambitious politicking that council elections bring to the big centres. It did. A charming difference too.

For example, although polling was less than a week away, there was absolutely no evidence whatsoever that anyone was campaigning, let alone canvassing. Maybe it's because of the ever-present Kakanuis. You see, the Maori name, literally translated, means "many parrots". So you had to watch what you said in those parts. False promises could well come back to haunt you.

Not that the place wasn't politically minded. No sir. It had a mayor and six councillors to administrate its fortunes. In 1974, the mayor, seventy-eight-year-old Harold Strode was standing unopposed for his third term of office. But there was competition for the council places. Nine candidates were contesting in fact. And that from a list of only sixty-seven local residents with the franchise. The total electoral roll in those days was swelled to a massive 220 by a host of absentee landowners. They were the bach or "crib" owners who put in an appearance during the holidays. Along with many others who found the place a delight to visit, they provided the lifeblood for the little community.

It hadn't always been like that of course. At one time, when it was known as Mount Ida, the town had serviced the needs of around 5000 people. That was when there was gold in the hills, back in 1863. However, it was a poor man's field and when the gold ran out by the turn of the century, so too did the miners. Apart from the ones that stayed on up at the top of the lane where the "no exit" sign was. They all left their mark though: the usual hideous sluicing scars around the town skirt; a curling rink; and a few old buildings, including "The Ancient Briton" pub and the Union church hall.

Built in 1865, the church hall was two years younger than the pub. Its corrugated iron cladding was and still is evidence of the fact. But never mind that its exterior is cold, its interior has provided warmth for thousands. As a Union church, it did, more than 100 years ago, what all the verbosity of diocesan councils fail to do today. It recognised its purpose. A place for people to worship in. Not a place to argue dogma. Presbyterians, Wesleyans, members of the Church of England, Bible Christians, Lutherans and Baptists all used it. And they all managed to kneel in the same pews without fighting. For a while anyway. Later the building became a school house. Now it's the local library.

The setting for this community must have been beautiful indeed before the gold rush. But even when I saw it, it had a unique quality. The sluice scars were rapidly disappearing, hidden by re-seeded larch trees. The curling rink, thank God, was bounded naturally by trees and not incarcerated by man's favourite plaything, the wire fence.

The main road which parts most of the town's little cottages, was tar-sealed it's true. But the harshness of that surface was softened by the green cricket field on one side and the fact that the artery was rarely used. Except when the mail arrived of course.

So quiet and solitary was that road, that I wanted to try to capture its quality in some way. I was lucky. The way presented itself.

It was early one afternoon. I was sitting by the side of the road eating a pie and chewing the fat over with my camera crew, when I saw him. Way off in the distance, an old man was walking along with his dog. Not another thing had moved along that road in hours. Immediately, I knew what I had to do. Within seconds, we had the camera up on the tripod, a telescopic lens on and an eye down the viewfinder.

Then we shot his progress down the street.

Next, when he'd reached a certain point, we rushed across and up the road to meet him. He'd probably never seen anyone else on the road at that time before, let alone three people running towards him with strange-looking pieces of equipment. He stopped in his tracks, his hand on the clog's leash tightening.

I explained who I was and what I was doing. He relaxed. Then we had the inevitable discussion about "the broadcasting". No one escapes it. For some reason, whenever the subject of filming for television is mentioned, the layman wants to tell you about some vague relation who works in "the broadcasting". Or at least, he'll give you a fairly comprehensive review of the current programmes and what he thinks of them. And the people in them. Over the years, I learned to accept it and tried to be patient. It wasn't always easy. Especially since I rarely watched television.

So, anyway, once I'd heard all about this guy's great nephew who was in the accounts section of NZBC Timaru, I got him to go back a few yards and repeat his final steps before I'd stopped him. After that, I came into the picture too, meeting him on camera, "spontaneously", and having a wee chat.

The interview wasn't all that important, because I had other plans for the sequence. However, we did learn one thing from the man. He was a bachelor, in his seventies, I discovered, and the little community contained a lot of widows. One of his fears it transpired, was that he'd get hooked by one of the ambitious ladies. You see, they apparently thought he was a good catch. Well, if he'd been single for seventy odd years, I suppose they reasoned that he'd been saving himself for Miss or Mrs Right. If not, at least there was a good chance he'd been saving.

Anyway, according to his story, he was the target for quite a few of the local females. Some of them even tried winning his interest with their cooking. He told us how they often turned up at his door with a tray of their home-baked cakes.

However, up until 1974, he'd managed to keep them at bay and retained his independence. He didn't say whether he'd sampled their cakes, though.

After he'd gone and the street was deserted again, we filmed me walking from the opposite direction, in a manner similar to the old man's. When the pieces were put together, I inter-cut between the two. First you saw the man and his dog, then me and so on, until we met in the middle of the town. I played the music from "High Noon" over the top.

The next morning, though, we really did see a high point of tension on the main street. The daily ritual for the townsfolk. At precisely 10.15 am each day, Alan Smith, the deputy mayor and proprietor of the store, brought in the mail. It was the last call on his round of deliveries that started when he dropped off milk and newspapers to the locals. After that, he transported high school pupils to Ranfurly, nine miles away and whilst there picked up Naseby's mail. Then he drove back, down the length of the borough's main street to the imposing brick post office, opposite the cricket ground.

For the next fifteen minutes, Naseby held its breath. Curtains at cottage windows, dropped back into place as peeping eyes withdrew. Nothing outside moved. Even sparrows froze. Inside the post office, the mail was being sorted.

Then it happened. Sharp on 10.30 am Naseby exhaled. A car came from that direction, a pair of feet from this. Two pairs of feet appeared from here and a bicycle and passenger from there. The town was on the move. And the people were all converging on the same spot. The post office.

Ten minutes tater, it was all over. The feet had moved off. The car had gone home. The cyclist had changed gear and was now slowly going back up the hill. The borough was settling back on its haunches. The main street was empty once more and it would stay that way until 10.30 the next morning.

Unless someone walked his dog. Or someone else slipped along to the store.

Incidentally, the store was the scene of one of the few issues of contention in the place. Particularly when holiday time came. That's when the locals became overwhelmed with the visitors and had their daily routine shattered.

They even had to queue for bread, would you believe. They didn't take too kindly to that at all. Why should they suddenly have to line up along with a load of strangers to get something they normally strolled along for every day of the week? It was a difficult problem for the politician-shopkeeper. Fortunately, or unfortunately, the locals had no choice.

The only other issues to plague the citizenry that I could discover were the need for a sewage treatment plant and some new chairs for the council chamber. There was fairly good support from the residents for both these moves. Particularly the replacement of the heavy wooden chairs. You see they were about 100 years old and not the most comfortable things made by man. Consequently, since none of the council members was getting any younger, it was either new chairs or shorter meetings.

Though what they met about, I can't conceive. Nor could one of the candidates. He was the publican of the rival hotel to the Ancient Briton. When I asked him why he was standing for election, he said: "To find out what goes on." It seems he was constantly being asked questions about the town by his customers, so he thought he'd get himself some authoritative answers.

However, I don't think he would have been much the wiser even with a seat at the council table. Outside of the sewage problem, things went along pretty smoothly in Naseby.

Oh, sure, they would have liked a resident policeman, or a doctor, but they did have a "day man". He was the one and only council employee in fact. And he was paid on a casual hourly rate. His duties included the ash collection and the town burying.

For one reason or another, most of the residents hoped that his workload would never get to the point where his job would become full-time.

I met a second "burying man" in another town in Otago that same year. The town was Queenstown and I was filming a pilot programme for a series I was to make the following year, "One Man's View".

The man who buried them in Queenstown was a little different from his Naseby counterpart, at least he was when I met him. For one thing, he wasn't employed by the council. He was a private undertaker. However, he did have a connection with the town's administrators - he was one of them. He'd been on and off the council for over thirty years in fact.

I was interested in talking to him more in his municipal role on local bodies, than in his funereal role of attending to local bodies. I had thought he would be my neutral opinion.

At the time, while Naseby was very much a shy and reluctant holiday centre, Queenstown was rapidly developing into a brash and ambitious tourist resort. Indeed already, more than a quarter of a million visitors were passing through the place every year. But this wasn't to everyone's liking, I learned.

There appeared to be a strong dichotomy of opinion if not of interests. Both sides of the argument of whether or not increasing development should take place, were represented on the council. I'd heard a few of the fors and againsts and now I sought the voice of reason.

It was true that my man, a Mr Les Lindsay, was also a fairly interested party. He was a builder as well as a burier, but, I'd heard that he was a man who spoke his mind. Unfortunately, though, he wouldn't do it for the camera. In fact he would hardly look up and talk to me when I approached him.

He was in his back garden in the middle of town. A tall, severe-looking man with close-cut grey hair and a pipe that looked as if it grew from his mouth, Les was gardening. His real love, I suspected. I have never seen such crops. Every bit of greenery above the ground looked gigantic. And so it should I suppose with the treatment it got. The entire surface of the earth was covered with a thick layer of sheep manure.

Also, I'd noticed from my motel room nearby, he had sprinklers drenching the stuff day and night. I dread to think what his veges actually tasted like.

Anyway, the only information I could get from the man was his comments on the state of the funeral business, as a result of Queenstown's burgeoning progress. Surprisingly, it wasn't all that good. Either they were passing through too quickly, or they were staying too long. I felt sorry for the chap. Still he did have his giant rank-smelling cabbages and silver beet.

That wasn't the only smell that was attached to him either, from what I gather. One of his colleagues on the council complained that he carried the strong aroma of embalming fluid with him to meetings. The lady concerned, a lover of fresh air and natural beauty reckoned that she was often asphyxiated by it.

The offended party was very aptly named Marigold. She was one of two lady councillors who formed the environmental bloc on the council. I gathered they had a difficult task. They were trying to stem what they considered was unnecessary and self-interested development and growth. Achieved, they claimed, at the expense of the town's natural beauty.

They had a few followers too. Some of the more affluent of the area would have liked Queenstown to stay as it always had been. Like a little Swiss settlement. It had the setting all right. Beautiful, freezing cold Lake Wakatipu and the Remarkables mountains with the challenging Coronet Peak right on their doorstep.

The other seven members of the council at the time were a little more pragmatic. They included Les the buryer, a retired food distributor, two moteliers, a land agent, a motelier/land agent and a motelier/land developer/restaurateur.

I suppose you don't need to be a Ralph Nader, to see why the majority of the council was fairly keen to encourage development. Well, it would be difficult to assemble such a group of qualified experts together anywhere. So why waste the expertise.

The two ladies, who followed their hearts though, were the flies in the ointment. The mayor, a Mr Warren Cooper, who was also a motelier/land agent, referred to them with obvious distaste as Flora and Fauna. Already in local body politics he was showing that rare flair for rhetoric and wit he was later to display in parliamentary debate.

Mr Cooper's philosophy was a simple, homespun one. Queenstown is so beautiful that it should be shared and enjoyed by everyone. I'm sure his dad "Wicked Willie", owner of the Hotel Queenstown would have raised his glass proudly to that if he'd been asked. Indeed I imagine that most people would find it hard to resist such generous openhearted sentiment. However a move to open up and develop more crown land at the back of the town wasn't so popular. Not with Marigold anyway. But then her opinion of her mayor and his motives were far from worshipful.

There was another chap in town, when I was there, who was very concerned about the state of the place. He was a young Australian named Peter Davies, a yoga master. He'd come to enlighten Queenstown, if Warren Cooper hadn't already done so. He called it one of the dirtiest towns he'd ever seen. From a spiritual viewpoint, I presume he meant. He was also worried about the people's bodies though. The locals didn't care about them at all, he said. I mentioned that I thought that Les the undertaker, was fairly concerned, but I soon discovered the Australian master had very little sense of humour.

Anyway, whether by coincidence or not, I noticed that all the participants in his class were female. So he'd either touched on some rich vein of vanity in the town or else he'd made sure in some way that they had been given the message.

The guy who let him use the church hall for his classes wasn't too impressed, though. The vicar I mean. That reverend soul called him Cassius's cousin and felt the yoga master had megalomania problems. He said he'd never before heard of people coming away from yoga classes with stiff backs.

There it was again. This slightly snide inference about each other. Everywhere you went you met it. Nobody seemed to trust another soul in the place. Not even the vicar. After all, the Australian yogi was doing whatever it was he was doing for free. He made his money working behind a bar in one of the hotels.

I've never been back to Queenstown since that time. I haven't really needed to. Even when I was there, the grossest kind of tourism was in full swing. The pre-packaged mass bus tours were sweeping in and out every twenty-four hours. One hotel manager was meeting plane groups, waving a little flag of their country, shepherding them in to a bus and whisking them off.

The beautiful place that everyone should share and enjoy was changing face. From something peculiarly New Zealand, to Tourist Town Anywhere. Only the kiwi trinkets, the greenstone tikis and the paua shell jewellery gave any clue to the land it was in.

I've seen the same collection of hotels and tourist treats the world over. From Tokyo to Toronto. From London to Los Angeles. Why tourists buy it I'll never know. Maybe some people collect visits to Ramada Inns the way I used to collect train numbers.

Mr Cooper, the former mayor, must have been proud of it all though. Particularly when he became Minister of Tourism in 1978. His star had shone ever brighter since his early days in the little alpine district. At one time, I'm told, he looked after the local camping ground there.

CHAPTER FIVE

The Coasters

AS SOON AS YOU GET TO the little township of Arthur's Pass in the middle of the great divide, you know you are leaving Canterbury and entering Westland. That's when the sandflies start biting. From then on, through the lush beauty of the National Park, you keep your eyes on the road and the windows of the car shut.

It doesn't take too long, even under those conditions, to realise that a change has occurred. The drivers coming towards you are taking the curves on your side of the road. They're all wearing trilbies on the backs of their heads and have cigarettes poking from the corner of their mouths. And they all lift one finger up from their hands on the steering wheels and wag it at you as they scream past.

That's right, you've hit the West Coast and seen your first West Coaster. So be warned. He's rough, he's tough, so he'll tell you, and he'll pull your leg atrociously if you let him. Like Mickey Neville, the moa man of Kumara. He was a mischievous seventy-year-old I met on my first visit to the coast in 1975.

Actually Kumara is about fifteen miles inland, but you're forced to go through it if you're headed for the main centres of Greymouth or Hokitika.

You're also forced to listen to Mickey too, if you happen upon him. He's a great talker, or he was in my day there. Mind you, the town is famous for producing great talkers. The most eloquent of them I suppose was the mighty King Dick, Richard John Seddon, the storekeeper-publican who lost a business but found his true calling in politics while living there. The toast of the coast, who became New Zealand's best-remembered Prime Minister, Dick Seddon was a thirty-one-year-old merchant when he turned up there.

He was one of the first to check out the place, when the cry of "gold" went up in 1876. A century later, Seddon was just a fond memory, but they were still dredging up a bit of gold from the Teremikau River at the back of the township.

That gave them something to talk about. Well, not a heck of a lot else happened in the little community of around 300 souls, where the priest was also the town constable. That's why the locals developed such a good gift for making up their own news. Like the moa story for instance.

It seems that someone had spotted some strange prints along the sandy banks of the river nearby. They looked as if they'd been made by a large bird's feet. They were different from anything anyone had seen before though.

The story was bandied around the pub bar. Mickey Neville was one of the interested listeners to the tale. Next day they all went to have a look. Sure enough, there were the very definite signs of a very large bird indeed. Along the beach the marks went and then off up into the bush.

Well there was only one bird that had feet that size and that had been extinct for centuries. Or had it? The seed of doubt had been cast. Probably by Mr Neville.

Anyway, the fascinated locals covered up the prints for the meantime and decided to check the area again later to see if any more appeared. Well of course they did.

Now the story was boiling. Soon it reached Greymouth and even beyond. Someone, somehow, had managed to relay the information to the University of Canterbury, where it came to the notice of a zoologist.

The next day, two experts in the study of New Zealand's famed bird of pre-history, the moa, arrived in Kumara. What had brought them no one knows. Maybe the coincidence of the prints associated with the name Kumara was too great for them to resist. As you may know, the last probable moa hunters were partial to the old sweet potato.

As it was, no trace of a living Dinorthiformes Moa had been found that could possibly establish its being extant after about 1300 AD. That's the big fellow by the way. It stood about three metres high according to photographs. However, they could have reasoned that there was still just a remote chance that one species the megalapteryx, had somehow survived.

There had been talk not too long ago that some of these characters could well still be hanging around Fiordland. Not that they were the real McCoy. The megalapteryx moa wasn't much more than a big kiwi. Standing, at the most, one metre from the ground. But even so, he could have big feet. Not only that, if he was a nocturnal creature like the kiwi, the theory could well be right. This mini-moa could have been hiding in the bush during the daytime and survived.

The experts took a look at the latest set of prints. They were very very interesting. Casts were made. The area was searched. There was something wrong though. Birds don't just fly. Moas, whether they are dinorthiformes or megalapteryxi, don't just walk. This was the topic that night in the pub. Again Mickey's twinkling eye and keen ear were amongst those gathered there.

The next day the bird hadn't just walked. It had dropped. Quite large samples had passed through its digestive system. Now the experts had something else to work on. Something tangible.

It was a master stroke. However, like so many master strokes, it was probably the trick that killed the canard. Maybe the false faeces didn't stand up to analysis. Anyway, the experts left as hurriedly as they'd arrived. Fortunately before they were laughed out of Kumara. And Mickey Neville couldn't play with his plaster reproduction of a moa's foot in the sand any more. Or mix up any more moa manure. But he did enjoy it while it lasted. Almost as much as he enjoys telling anyone and everyone about it.

The town fed off that hoax for ages.

But although a Coaster likes a good laugh at another's expense, he does tend to over-react to any kind of criticism of either himself or the Coast.

For instance, it's not wise to mention the rain whilst you're over there. Even if the town of Greymouth is awash from the flooded banks of the river Grey, a local will deny it's raining. He'll tell you it's just a mist that comes over the hill from Runanga. And the biting wind that screams down to the streets from the upper Grey valley is only a breeze, despite the fact that it cuts in so fiercely, it's known as the "barber".

Yessir, the Coaster is a stubborn person whatever his sex too. And some things really upset him. As I discovered when we started filming there.

We were in a Greymouth back street, just about to shoot some film of an ancient house. It had gained my interest because it was almost obliterated from view by plant growth. Trees, bushes, vines were guarding it like jailers round a dangerous criminal. The shot was intended to illustrate a bit of whimsy, nothing more.

Anyway, the camera was up on the tripod, but just as the cameraman was about to push the button and roll, the high fence behind us opened up. We hadn't even noticed the gate.

"You're not going to film that old place, are you?" An old lady in a pinafore, with her teeth out and her hair tucked in a kerchief was standing, thin-eyed, behind us.

"As a matter of fact we are, why?" I don't like to be interrupted too much when I'm working, but I tried to sound polite.

"What on earth do you want to do that for? That old dump. There's plenty of nice homes in Greymouth without picking that one. There's no one living there, it looks awful. You people are all the same, just trying to give Greymouth a bad name. Like that Brian Edwards. All he did was to come over here and try to show us up." She took a breath. Just long enough for me to get in and tell her that nothing could be further from my mind. I assured her that I had no intention whatsoever of disparaging the wonderful town. All I wanted, I said, was to show the bountiful plant life that existed on the coast.

"Oh, well, there's plenty of that all right. But don't try to give us a bad name, that's all..." and she went muttering back through the hole in the fence.

Many years before this, Brian Edwards, as a television reporter, had done a bit of filming on the coast for the Christchurch programme "Town and Around". The locals had never forgotten it.

Later that day, we bought some petrol from one of the garages in town. The proprietor spotted the filming equipment in the back of the car. He raised the subject. This time threats were included. "If that Brian Edwards character ever shows his face over here again, he'll regret it. He'll get beaten up!" the man said.

They really were angry. I assumed that the reporter had ripped the place apart with ascerbic comment and criticism for some reason or other. That he had vented his spleen on this odd little corner of the world. But no. He'd committed a much worse crime. He'd actually done an interview with someone on the beach.

Ironically, I don't think the subject of the interview, although no doubt controversial, was in any way responsible for the local ire. It was the location. The beach in Greymouth quite often is literally piled up with driftwood. It is a perfectly natural and understandable occurrence. The Tasman sea can be pretty turbulent at times. However, it could quite fairly be said that because of the action of the tides, the beach can be made to look a little unsightly. Not your Palm Beach, Florida, you might say. On that particular occasion, it looked positively grotty. And the coasters will never forgive Mr Edwards for showing it.

It's all a bit of a paradox really. This apparent concern for their image, to the outsider. Because in my experience there is no other part of New Zealand that is so fiercely independent and determined to retain its individuality.

Some even go so far as to say that while the South Island may talk seriously about the advantages of secession from New Zealand, the West Coast has never really joined.

Certainly, the Coasters have a reputation for not paying great heed to all the rules and regulations that pour forth from the oracle in Wellington. Indeed a Wellington bureaucrat is almost as abhorrent to the people of Westland as a worthy conservationist. Particularly one who wants to stop the coal from being mined or the trees from being milled. That's like cutting their economic throat. They feel they've bled enough.

But don't get me wrong. I don't want to suggest that they're a dour people, far from it. Perhaps just a little sensitive to outside interference. I'm sure they'd all agree with that. No, on second thoughts, I'm not so sure they would. In fact, I'm not confident that anyone should dare to make any kind of definitive statement. Either about the Coast or the people who live there. You see a great many of the. inhabitants are of Irish descent and the logic that prevails there is straight from the Emerald Isle. Once you recognise the kind of rules they operate by, however, everything starts to drop into place. You can begin to understand some of the slightly idiosyncratic behaviour you often encounter over there.

Like the time we considered doing a bit of filming on Dunollie railway station. Sitting on top of a hill overlooking the coal town of Runanga, this is not the busiest station on the Coast, but a vital one. Vital to the men who worked in the Strongman mine up the line in the hills.

I was considering shooting the miners returning from work, alighting from the train and making their way down the hill to their homes. A simple enough shot, to cut in with filming to be done at the mine face. The crew and I thought we should take a look first at the specific routine that was followed.

The train was due in at 2.30 pm so we got there about a quarter-past-two. I wanted to talk with the station master first to get all the facts. He wasn't there. Nobody was. The place was deserted. So we waited.

There wasn't a lot to see. The station building was a two-roomed wooden shed. One room for the public, the other for the staff. It had just the one platform and a jump down from that, one rail. To the left, it wound up a slope and away round a corner to be lost in the bush. To the right was a separate rail or siding and all the handles that go with a simple junction and switching operation. And that was that. In front of us the high clay bank topped by bush stared back blankly.

All was still. Only the cicadas shrilled from hiding places.

At 2.26, we heard the rumble of a train from the hills to the left. At 2.28 it stopped. Probably just around the corner from our view. It was standing by, waiting for a sign. It sounded its siren.

No answer came from the station. How could it? No one was there, apart from my crew and me. At 2.31 the train horn was louder and more persistent. It was anxious to get in and deposit its passengers. They'd been working since 5 am and were thirsty.

Nothing moved. Even the cicadas seemed to hold their breath. You could feel the silence. At 2.33 the stillness was broken. Suddenly a roaring six cylinder cloud of dust came up the hill from the township below. It swerved into the car park behind the station and screamed to a stop.

Within seconds, a young man with a shock of gingery curly hair, a check, open-necked shirt and a railwayman's uniform on, leapt past us and down on to the track. First he pulled a couple of handles there, then he hoisted himself back on to the platform, unlocked the staff door and disappeared.

From outside, we heard a series of sharp, clicking sounds followed by ringing bells, before the door flew open and out he came again. This time, he sped past us in the other direction to pull some more mysterious handles at the side of the little building. While he was doing this, the glowing headlight of the train had slowly shone its way around the corner and was tentatively heading for the platform. Already men were hanging out of open doors poised ready to leap off. As soon as it was alongside, leap they did and run. Five or ten seconds later, the train was empty and the men had all vanished. Only the camera crew, myself and the station master remained. But for a pause only.

Then our red-headed friend was all action again. Leaping back onto the tracks, he pulled a couple more of the handles, hoisted himself up again and vanished into his room of clicks and bells. The single carriage train slid gently out of view. And that was that. The station master's work was over for the day. But why wasn't he there before the train arrived? And where had he dashed from? Why, the pub of course. He'd been down with the boys, having a jar and a sandwich. Didn't notice the time, would you believe.

Even so, he wouldn't have got away as quickly as he did, if he'd been part of the company at another pub I heard about.

The pub was in a place called Blackball, another little coal town a bit further up the Coast. Well it had been a coal town. When I went there though it was really considered more of a ghost town although there were signs indicating that it was coming back. Many of its old cottages had been bought up by dropouts who'd dropped in, or people commuting to work in Greymouth. However any real future prosperity depended on whether proposals to mine nearby Mt Davy came off or not.

As it was the local mine workings were long since abandoned. But the pub was still there and there was a community. Mostly Irish. The total population in 1975 was just over 300. Twenty-one of those were widows.

In all West Coast towns the pub is the social centre. The drinking habits are still very much like the British ones. The pub is where you meet your friends, play some darts or billiards and hold your wakes or parties.

The Coaster takes this part of his life very seriously. Nothing is allowed to interfere with the fun whilst a party is in progress. Not even death. It's an inconvenience, but it should never be an interference. Well that's what I gathered from a story told to me about a party at the Blackball pub one time.

It was a lively affair apparently, a wedding I believe, and the toasts were still being made five hours after the meal had finished.

The fiddler was there, the jigs were being danced and everyone was having the time of their lives. Then one of the old timers dropped dead. It was most untimely. But it wasn't allowed to interrupt the festivities.

However, with the dancing going on, they couldn't leave the body where it had dropped. At the same time, nobody was too keen to take it away either. So, they sat it up on the bar, leaning against the post.

Well, the party went on, the beer flowed freely, the dancing got merrier and merrier and the fellow propped up on the bar was completely forgotten. Until his jaw fell open and a full set of teeth fell out. That sobered the scene up a trifle.

It was one of those horrible moments of truth that you can't ignore, however drunk you may be. The teeth were on the floor, the man was on the counter. Was there any point in picking them up and returning them to their owner? The question was on a lot of their minds although they all realised of course that he wouldn't be doing a heck of a lot with them in future, that's for sure.

A decision had to be made. The body was beginning to slide down the bar post. Before too long, he'd make up their minds for them. He'd be down on the floor with his teeth. Anyway, now that they'd had to stop, some of the men decided to take the old fellow outside and stick him in the back of a car. Just for the meantime. Then they all went back to the party.

It didn't take more than another couple of rounds of booze and a jig or two before everything was back in full swing. And so it went on all night and well into the wee hours of the morning.

The following day, everybody agreed it had been one of the best shindigs ever. That was when the seltzers and aspirins had done their work. But then someone remembered the old chap they'd left in the back of the car. Nobody had given him a thought when the party finally broke up.

Eventually, it seems, that a couple of the more responsible members of the community decided to do the decent thing. They returned to the pub to pick up the body and deliver it to the local undertaker. However when they got there, it was gone. When they opened up the car they'd left it in, the corpse was no longer in it.

To this day, no one knows where it went. Or how it went. I suspect it walked. After putting its teeth in, I hope.

Stories connected with the drinking habits of the Coaster are legion. In fact most of the humour there is based on booze in one way or another.

They have their own licensing hours for one thing.

While pubs throughout the rest of New Zealand are closed on Sunday, the coast pubs are unofficially, officially open. Provided you don't make it known of course. Most publicans over there have an arrangement with the local police sergeant. In most cases, the officer will turn a blind eye. Just as long as the unofficial drinking is kept to the official times- but that's unofficially official, you realise.

Every coaster that can stand will tell you it's not so. That it's a lot of lies. But then he'll also deny that you can get a drink after hours during the week by giving three taps on the back door.

I think the funniest sight on the coast is a pub on a Sunday. During the unofficial official hours, I mean. You can see it's not open by all the cars parked around the place. The windows are all shut tight and the curtains drawn. The front door is locked. If you knock, you won't get an answer. It is playing at being dead. However if you put your ear to the window, you can hear the sounds of bar conviviality. And if you slip around the back and give the correct signal, you can join in.

The irony is that everyone knows all about it. Yet the Coasters will swear on the unofficial glass in his hand that it just isn't so.

I don't know how often the local police pay an impromptu visit these days, but at one time, after hours drinkers had to be constantly on the alert. With good reason. When the rest of the country had six o'clock closing, the Coasters went home around eleven. Unless the pub was raided that is. Like one I heard about that struck a really bad patch.

I'm not too sure just where this particular hostelry was

located, but it doesn't really matter. The only relevant identifying point was the local fish and chip shop across the road. You see, business in that establishment was bad. So bad indeed that the owner, a widow in her middle years, was forced to use desperate measures to get customers.

Now everyone knew that three taps at the back door got you in to the pub, no matter what the hour. Some people also knew that a certain combination of knocks on the front door was a warning for you to get out. The police were on the way. So, when that knock came, everyone made a dash for the back door and the nearest refuge until the danger was over.

The fish frying widow knew the routine as well as anyone. So, when the business was at rock bottom, she decided to act. Over the road she went. Tap, tap, tap she knocked on the front door and back to her shop she raced. It wt>rked a treat. Sure enough, out the back door, along the shadows and across the road they came in their scores. No longer was there fish lying around battered and unwanted. The business picked up exceptionally after that. Well it seems the police had it in for that pub opposite. The raids kept coming at least twice a week.

That was in the good old days, of course, when mum was in the kitchen and dad was "down to the pub". When he wanted to at that. The Coaster's view was that a man should get a drink when he's thirsty, not when some dessicated public servant decrees.

Things have changed a bit since then though. I'm told that when licensing hours were extended from six o'clock to ten o'clock throughout the nation, the West Coast went along with that. They apparently didn't mind losing an hour to fall in line. Even so, there are doubtless some exceptions. Certainly the Coaster has never been happy with a lot of what he sees as anomalies in the law.

One of the most outspoken on the subject that I came across, was the publican of the Cobden pub in Greymouth. I filmed him in his bright and busy bar.

"Listen, I've had some run-ins with the law, I can tell you."
"What for?"
"What? ...After hours trading. The last time my bloody dog's name was taken." Just then he had to break off to serve one of the many men sitting up at the bar and have a joke with another one. He was a character.

Ron Thompson was a short, slightly built man in his fifties, I would think. He wore his dark hair cut short at the back and sides with a parting and he had a cheeky smile hovering on his lips. His eyes were hidden behind strong, horn-rimmed glasses. His air was jaunty and his voice gravelly from the barroom smoke.

He was back again, leaning confidentially forward. "For instance, I can't entertain you in the bar after a quarter-past-ten at night. My mother-in-law has lived here with my wife and me for twelve years. She could entertain us because she's a boarder here. We couldn't entertain her. Now that is an anomaly... This has got to be faced..."

Mr Thompson had been serving and sipping for quite a few hours. He wasn't going to be an easy man to keep to the subject I could see. I wanted to know more about the little gem he'd thrown out just before though.

"What happened with the dog?" I reminded him.

"Well, we were listening to the Apollo 11 finding its way back to earth's orbit... and we were confronted by a sergeant who..." At that point, my sound operator cut in to tell me he hadn't heard the line because of the noise in the bar. So we had to reposition the microphone and start again.

"Yes, OK Ron, what happened when you were summonsed?"

"Well, we were sitting down in the... in the sitting room. In our private sitting room and a ring came to the doorbell. So I looked at the phone." His eyes twinkled and he looked around to his audience. "Got up and answered the door and in came the sergeant. And he said to John (presumably a guest) 'what are you doing down here in the private sitting room?'" Ron emphasised the last three words. "Well, he reckoned he saw us come out of the bar, which was bullshit. He didn't see us come out of the bar, because we weren't in the bloody bar. As was proved by the magist... by the court. They all got off but he took my dog's name." He was off down the bar again, joking and pouring. I was beginning to wonder if I'd ever get the story finished.

When he came back this time, I tried to tie him down. The piano was going now in the background and it was getting very noisy. I leaned over the bar: "Took your dog's name? How did that happen?" "Well, I tell you what." He was enjoying the memory. "It's funny really. He (the sergeant) took everyone's name down, you see, and then he said: 'is there anyone else's name to be taken?' Oh, yes, I said, there's one little black fella knocking around here. You haven't seen him, but he's probably seen you. 'Who is he?' says the sergeant officiously. Brendwar Rogal, I said. He wrote the name down in his book. so, when we got to court... seven people appeared in court charged with being in here after hours. But there were eight names. The magistrate said: 'Would you read those names out again, Sergeant please?' So he read them out again. 'Well,' said the magistrate, 'there appears to be eight and only seven appeared.' Then he appealed to my solicitor: 'Ah, how many clients have you got Mr Mcginnley?' 'Seven,' said Mcginnley. 'But there are eight names here.' 'Well', he said 'close the court, we'll work this out and ah, come back at three o'clock in the afternoon.' Which we all did. Well, everybody got off, you see, bar Robby (his wife) and me. We were fined heavily. And this Brendwar Rogal... When they read Brendwar Rogal's name out in court this time, my wife got up and said, 'But you can't have him, he's my dog.' The magistrate said 'clear the court!' "

"The case was dismissed?" I queried.

"No. Dismissed, no, Christ no. We were fined. We were gonna be put in jail because we wouldn't pay the fine."

"But they let the dog off?" "Oh, yes. Oh they let him off! But now listen, in Ireland, in Ireland, if a farmer doesn't give

103

a pig a drink seven days a week, he's before the court. And in New Zealand if you give a man a drink on a Sunday and he's caught, well I'm caught too... there's another anomaly isn't it?"

I left Ron to lecture and entertain his customers with that strange logic. He was just getting warmed up. That's what brought them in I suspect.

Although it wasn't what brought one customer in to that particular pub. No it was the whisky. The Cobden just happened to be this man's nearest source.

His name was Jimmy Rhodes. The Coasters had dubbed him "Dusty" shortly after he arrived there from Christchurch in 1920. Apparently, one of those stubborn folk, ignoring the rain that poured down on them while they talked, said: "It doesn't rain much over here y'know. It's usually dusty like you, dry." The name stuck and "Dusty" Rhodes had lived there ever since.

He was eighty-four years old when I found him. Painting at an easel in his cosy front room in a neat little house down the road from the pub.

Just about everyone in Greymouth either owned or had seen a sample of Dusty's talent with the brush. Indeed anyone who ever passes through that town has. For one thing, the official sign on the roadside at the town's entrance was painted by him. Then there are murals in the RSA building, the local convent and literally stacks of his art in the storeroom of the local operatic society.

He called it his hobby, if anyone asked. Because he didn't want to jeopardise his pension, he said. However he must have made a few bob on the side. "It pays for the good juice" was how he explained it.

Mr Rhodes was quite an amazing old painter. A thin, wiry chap, with a "scrooge" bed cap on, he made an interesting sight dabbing away at his canvas. Most fascinating though was the fact that his right arm, his painting arm, shook quite vigorously between dabs. He'd suffered some kind of nervous injury during service in World War One. It had left the limb with a permanent shake. But only, it appeared, when it wasn't in active use.

Well, Dusty had certainly given it some use over the years. And not just from painting. He'd lifted more glasses than palettes, I suspect. But he'd also been a hairdresser. In fact hairdressing had been his trade, despite the fact that he'd been to art school in Christchurch. He'd even had a patron in his youth. A solicitor in that city used to buy his paintings. Dusty said the man only did it because he felt sorry for "the poor little bugger".

However in spite of that early encouragement, until he retired from barbering, his art had always taken second place. There was obviously more money in hair oil than there was in oil paint. Some of the tips were quite good too, especially when he worked in Burman's hair salon in Wellington's Lambton Quay. That apparently was the barber shop most patronised by the nation's legislators.

"One customer was Sir Joseph Ward. He had a slight... pimply thing on his face," said the old man, "so I used to doctor it up and trim his moustache. Put a little wax on it and make him look nice. And I always got a ten bob tip."

Nothing is sacred is it. Just imagine all the stories that barbers could tell about parliamentarians. They do tell them of course, but they can't be printed. Not until they've been locked up in the archives for fifty years.

But it was Dusty's painting that I was interested in and the prolific way he turned the pictures out.

A Lake Matheson or a Mount Cook from memory took about three or four hours to complete. Depending on the amount of "liquidation" he got from the "juicery", as he put it. Then there was the really big stuff. Even at eighty four, he was on hand, if called, to paint the scenery for the operatic society. With his feet sometimes. He used to dip his feet in the paint pot and walk across to make giant leaves.

However, the money was in the landscapes. For the locals, he would practically give them away for about ten dollars. But the tourists had to pay more. Particularly the Americans.

He told me how the publican sent visitors along to him and how he used to "sting the Yankees" with prices of $30 and $40 a piece.

Dusty was a shrewd old devil and although he didn't really qualify to be called a Coaster (your parents have to have been born there) he was every bit as independent. He'd given up the "meals on wheels" service to pensioners when he was about eighty-two because he found the food boring. He did all his own cooking, including baking scones of course. I didn't get a chance to sample them when I was there, but I was offered some of his "dry" humour.

We'd been talking about his ancestry and how he came from a line of long-livers; his mother was ninety-two when she died. I mentioned that I'd heard he came from quite a distinguished family.

"Oh, well, yes," he said, drawing noisily on his empty pipe, "Sir Roland Hill, you know, brought the penny post in."

"Who was he?" I fed him, as the straight man.

"He was my great-grandfather!" he answered proudly, but obviously not finished.

"Your great-grandfather?" I repeated. I assumed I was meant to.

"Yes," said Dusty, a hurt tone now entering his voice, "but he left me no money." He'd set me up, so I asked the vital question. "Why was that then?"

The old artist could hardly wait, he was practically bursting to deliver the punch line: "I wasn't born yet!" At which he let out a roar of laughter. I'll never learn.

I had to play straight man again a couple of days later. That's when I talked to a certain Basil Piner, fisherman, contractor, entrepreneur and fish processor. He's also an eloquent spokesman for the local fishing industry and one of the drivers you could meet coming at you on your side of the road somewhere between Canterbury and the Coast. He'll be taking his fish to market. Very fast indeed.

Physically, a very big man, Mr Piner is a West Coast character with a difference. He can't abide an apathetic attitude to anything. He's very positive. A self-made man who doesn't believe in relying on anyone and he usually says what he thinks. But rarely without humour.

We were standing near to the end of the finger jetty on the north side of Greymouth harbour. Above us morose clouds were just sitting there, threatening. A few feet away, curling surf was pounding the rock and cement escarpment that keeps the sea where it belongs. The wind was sharp and the spray was stinging, but Basil insisted that the scene was dead calm. I was interviewing him about the dangers for fishermen from the treacherous sandbar at the entrance to the harbour. In the past, ships have come to grief on it, and even the fishing boats have problems sometimes both going out and coming in.

Maybe a particularly lean time will force a fisherman to risk trouble on the bar by leaving port in bad weather or high sea. But in those circumstances it is his choice. However if he's out there fishing and the weather turns sour, he's got no choice at all. He's got to come home somehow, sandbar or no sandbar. There's no other place to shelter in for a hundred miles along that coast.

The whole subject was a serious one, but this Coaster dealt with it lightly. I asked him whether there was danger at the harbour mouth all the time. I was almost seasick just standing there looking at the turbulence.

"No", said Basil, "not all the time. Some days we get some good patches and some real sticky patches. You know it gives you concern like when the sea comes away and the boats are out there. This jetty here is lined with anxious people, until the last moment. 'Til they're all in."

He was being serious then.

"Would this be the most dangerous bar along this coast?" I knew that Hokitika, although no longer used as a port, also had a treacherous sandbar at its mouth. I also knew of the traditional rivalry between the two centres. Basil ignored the inference completely.

"Yes, I would imagine it would be. This one stops them

from getting in, and the one up town stops them from getting out. So they've got some serious problems down there."

Now I was back into the routine. Feeding the straight lines.

"That's used quite frequently, isn't it? I mean the bar. In bad weather?" It proved to be the right line.

"Actually," retorted Basil, "there's more fish caught up there than there is out here. Trouble is we've got no sale for it."

"But what about the dangers of that sandbar, Basil, for the tuna people for instance?" I wanted to get back to the point.

The fisherman was serious once more: "Well, we've had some worrying times, scary sort of times. Actually only the laundry knows how scary they have been at times."

I knew I'd probably regret it, but I had to experience crossing that sandbar for myself. Whatever the result. It's either a terrible curiosity I have, or else a touch of masochism. Particularly in this case. I am a lousy sailor. I once crossed the Atlantic from Liverpool to Halifax in Nova Scotia and threw up every day of the voyage. Still I had to know what the feeling of crossing a sandbar in a small fishing craft was like. After all, Basil Piner had assured me that the sea was dead calm.

So, the big man of the sea arranged to take me out. I felt confident with him on board. Not only because he was an experienced boat handler, but because he wouldn't want to take any risks. You see, although he must have been fast approaching sixty, I'd heard that Basil was soon to become a father again. As he explained it to me:

"Well, I changed boats in mid-stream, you might call it. My ex-wife got married again and I got married again and I have a youngster coming along. I hope to get the old age pension and the child allowance all in one. Then I can really go to the pub and shout for the boys when they're having a hard time."

Nothing could go wrong with a guy like that along, could it. Even so, as I clambered onto a fifteen-foot fishing boat, riding against the wharf side, I began to have my doubts. Especially when my sound operator refused to board.

This was a new situation. Mutiny on land. I'd never had to deal with insubordination like this before. I wanted to film and record not only the passage of the boat going over the sandbar, but my reaction to the experience. Particularly when we hit the real sea on the outside of the narrow harbour channel. I'd also wanted to keep talking to Basil on the way. However, the fact that my filming plans were being jeopardised, suddenly wasn't as important as the effect on me that this sound recordist's recalcitrance was having. Cowardice is contagious.

But I was too far in this one to turn back. So I cursed his parentage and we sailed without him. We somehow managed to set the sound recording equipment up so that the unit manager could operate it instead.

As things turned out though, there was little to record. Basil hadn't been joking when he said it was dead calm. Exaggerating a wee bit, but not pulling my leg. Indeed, I almost had to act out a feeling of fear and trepidation at the vital moment of the crossing.

Maybe the seamanship was too proficient. Because even though the bow of the boat was ducking and rising a fair bit, the experience was well short of my expectations. The cameraman must have felt the same way too. I noticed he was waving the camera up and down to add some dramatic effect to the scene. Although I must say when we did hit the open sea the story was a little different. It didn't take too long out there for me to realise that we'd all be seeing what I had for breakfast if we hung around.

I wasn't sorry when Basil agreed to my suggestion that I had better get back to do some more urgent filming that I had lined up.

Actually, I had a date with a lady. About two hours later. But not to film. Well not until I'd done some research and sounded her out. So, the sound operator, skulking guiltily in the shadows when we returned wouldn't be needed again.

My appointment was with one of two very independent Westland ladies we found. Both of them living in remote spots that had once been bustling boom areas. The first, a Mrs Merewether, had for most of the previous ten years been the sole resident of the former gold town of Stafford. Her house sat up on top of a knoll near the entrance to the abandoned site. When I went to see her in 1975, she had new neighbours down the road a little way. A young American couple were living in one of the old houses left, producing honey. Well the bees they kept were.

Mrs Merewether, a delicate, frail lady of seventy-four sometimes still rode her horse about ten miles or so to take afternoon tea in Hokitika. The horse's name I learned was Winnie and for some reason she used to give it and her twelve year old sheep Dorian, peppermints to suck. I never did find out why, but I don't think she would have told me if I'd asked her. She was terribly shy and extremely dignified.

Her home, humble as most on the Coast, was a spotless museum of memories. Sadly though, she wouldn't release any of them to the public. Try as I may, I couldn't get the lady to appear on camera.

I had a reason for urging this lady of the hill to change her mind. Not just because she was normally the only person living in a lonely, desolate ghost town. But because of the key role she played in the sub-plot. And that's not in any way meant as a pun. You'll see what I mean in a minute.

Just down the road from Mrs Merewether's house of peppermints was the Stafford cemetery. An exclusive burial ground in a beautiful bush setting. Amongst the gravestones, Richard Seddon had seen two of his infant children prematurely placed alongside his uncle Nathan. Presumably, they were all Stafford residents. That was the qualification to get in there by the 1970s anyhow. In fact, at the time that I met her, Mrs Merewether would be the last. The cemetery was going to be closed. The council had left just the one plot. They were waiting for her.

The other lady of Westland I bumped into on my travels, like "Dusty" Rhodes wasn't a true Coaster, despite her forty-nine years in the area. She was from Auckland. But she showed more grit, wit and gumption than most of the men in those parts.

I found her quite by chance. I was on my way to Waiuta, yet another abandoned mining area, like Stafford, that had at least one resident left. He was a famous old chap by the time I got to know about him. Almost a tourist attraction.

However, a couple of miles or so before we arrived at Waiuta to do some initial reconnoitring, we made a stop at a place called Blackwater. It was no more than a fistful of houses really. That's all that was there. No shops. For once, no pub. Heaven only knows what the ten residents did with their leisure time.

Anyway, we'd been driving some time along the back country roads and had become a little doubtful of our directions. The area was well away from Greymouth where we'd been filming, and nearer to Reefton. So, we felt we'd better stop and ask the way.

We pulled up outside the first house we saw. There was an official looking sign nailed up to the left of the front door: Telephone. It was the local post office. I soon discovered it was also the home of seventy-eight year-old widow, Nellie Fellowes, or 'Aunt Nell' to everyone who knew her.

Within five minutes of meeting, I'd arranged to come back and film her. And it wasn't just her offer to bake scones for us all that did it. No, Nell was a natural, for television, I mean. She was interesting to look at, colourful to talk to, completely relaxed with strangers and she had something to say.

She was a biggish woman with the sad look of the comedian. Her grey hair was short and curled and her grey-green eyes were magnified by strong lenses in round gold rimmed spectacles. At first glance she appeared almost brusque in her manner. Someone who would stand for no nonsense. But Nell really had all the quaint charm of a typical grandmother. She made me feel comfortable in her presence from the time I met her. She also made me laugh.

Not only did the lady have a keen wit, but she also had a repertoire of very funny jokes.

Nellie Fellowes had come to Blackwater to join her family in 1929. And what a family it must have been. Twelve children. There had been thirteen born in fact, but one had died from meningitis.

Both her parents were originally from England. Dad, a cockney, was a tinsmith by trade and a miner by necessity. He'd worked in quartz mines in Thames, in the Coromandel and in something else in the Bay of Plenty. Then in 1915, he'd brought his wife and children to the West Coast to see what the mines offered there. And that's when the family first entered the post office business.

At that time, there were a few hundred people in the district and the post office had been run by a local girl. A little irresponsibly, I gather.

It seems that this particular postmistress developed a bad habit. By all accounts she was an excellent saleslady: she sold all the stamps the main post office sent her. She even kept requesting that they send her more. Unfortunately though she must have been a lousy banker. Because she never sent any money in return. So she had to go.

Coincidentally, one of Nellie's sisters was due to leave school. The family applied for the post office for her. Three years later, when that girl left to get married, father was officially appointed postmaster of Blackwater. At five pounds one and seven pence a calendar month.

Officially, Nellie's dad remained in the job until he died in 1952 at the age of eighty-six. He even had an official testimonial presented to him in 1949 for thirty-one years' faithful service. In actual fact though, it was his wife who was selling most of the stamps. Dad was also down the mine for much of his time.

However, he kept in touch with the authorities. A bit too much I would think for their liking. You see he would keep pestering them for a raise. He was battling against a pretty inflexible master though. The public service book of rules said he wasn't entitled to more. Indeed when they checked and discovered he'd been getting a total of sixty pounds a year, they informed him that he was already paid over scale.

The cockney tinsmith was adamant and it paid off. Finally after a considerable exchange of correspondence, he received a letter signed by the Director General. It said that although no increase was officially due, in view of his long service to the post office, his salary would be raised to seventy-five pounds per annum. That was in 1951. The following year he died. So mum reaped the benefit of his persistence. She took over officially as postmistress at the age of seventy-seven.

My gosh they must have been a nuggety family. Nellie's mother carried on doing the job until she was eighty-five. Then finally and reluctantly, she handed over the reins to a youthful Nell, then a mere sixty-three. Nellie had been doing the job ever since. With only one raise granted since her battling father had squeezed one out back in 1951.

Mind you, the job was a bit easier in Nell's day. For one thing the office no longer handled money. Well, they paid so little, I suppose they didn't want to tempt the postmistress. Not that Nell would have been tempted. She was straight down the line.

We filmed her first from the outside of her little four-roomed cottage. She was waiting on the wooden verandah, two stone steps up from a lawn sprinkled with jonquils.

"Are you there?" I was walking up the garden path. In more ways than one.

"Right here," came the strong voice from the doorway.

"How are you?"

"Very good, thanks."

"I hear you've been sick."

"Yes, my privilege." Who'd dare argue with this lady.

"Your privilege, is it? Not too serious, though, is it?"

"No. Only pleurisy."

"Pleurisy? That's not too good."

Nell was standing by the post at the top of the steps as I climbed up. she was wearing a floral blouse, a light brown cardigan and a pair of trousers. One hand was free to give me a heave up, I noticed.

"Fortnight on holiday, in hospital, it was marvellous," she said, straight-faced.

It would have been a rest for her anyway. Although I imagine that they had to strap her into an ambulance to get her there. She was as tough as the timbers holding up her tin roof. She'd had to be. And she'd been used to working for quite a while. It was not surprising that her hands were as big as a man's. A manual working man's at that.

Her first jobs came when she was still at school. As a twelve-year-old she'd started by looking after other people's children. Later she'd cleaned houses and hung wallpaper, among other things. She hadn't joined the rest of the family until she was in her early thirties, still a single and single-minded young woman.

In Blackwater she met her husband, a blacksmith who liked his booze. A little too much, averred Nellie, who claims she built their house in the township with her own hands. I can believe it too. As I mentioned, those hands weren't made for crocheting. Although she could do that as well.

In fact there appears to be little that Aunt Nell couldn't do or didn't try. Apparently she lined up with the men in the creek where the family had a small gold claim. That's not the most pleasant of tasks under ideal conditions. On the West Coast though the gold seeker was under continual harassment from the vicious sandflies while he panned.

Nellie told me how, when she was working down there with her sleeves pulled down as far as possible, she'd suddenly realise she had a black bracelet around her wrist. It was sandflies, massed and feeding. When she washed them away, her wrist would be covered in blood. All for four ounces a week of the glistering stuff. Mind you that would be worth a few sandfly bites right now.

When I knew her, the old postmistress of Blackwater had given up working the claim. In fact she was looking for someone to buy it, along with her house and the two acres of land it stood on. She reckoned she wanted to move back north. Her daughter and grandchildren lived in Auckland and she wanted to be a bit nearer to them. But not too near. Nell didn't like the city too much. She was planning on spending her last days in the Coromandel.

She would be leaving an idyllic scene. Her verandah looked across the road to nothing but paddocks and bushclad hills. The air was as clean as the floor of her house and the bird songs carried right through the valley. But Nell wanted out. She'd decided that she was getting too old to keep chopping down trees for her firewood and scything an acre or so of lawns around the place. Her post office work wasn't going to hold her back either. That's for sure. She regarded it with a fair bit of cynicism:

"All they gave me was a telephone. They didn't even give me a desk to write on."

"Really?"

"They asked me whether I would take the office and I said yes. I asked what sort of building am I getting and they said you're not. Where will we put the telephone?' So I said, stick it by the front door. And that's all I got."

"But I suppose you get all the privileges of the civil servant... free telephone calls?" I suggested.

She was indignant: "Oh, nothing of that sort, no, nothing free."

"Why is that?"

"I don't know. I don't even get paid holidays. If I get somebody to take over, I have to pay them." I detected a slightly bitter tone that must have been inherited from Dad.

"Yes, but then I expect you're always on the phone to your mates up the road." There were three other houses still left with people living in them. They were about a hundred yards further along the road from Nell's place.

Her face lengthened in a frown: "Oh, no, I can't get them without paying a toll."

"What?" I suddenly had the feeling I was throwing those straight lines again. "They're on another exchange. This telephone," she pointed one huge finger at the instrument on the wall, "connects with Reefton and Greymouth. That's my head office. And when I ring 'Tolls' I get Greymouth. And if I want to ring next door, I've got to go through Reefton, Greymouth and Ahaura... to ring next door," she repeated.

Just so you get the picture quite clear. Reefton is about eighteen miles away from Blackwater. Greymouth about thirty and tiny Ahaura approximately fifteen. The house she would be calling, remember, was almost within shouting distance.

"At the expense of twenty-seven cents," she added with a smile.

"To ring your mates up the road." I emphasised.. "To ring up the road. If I cut me foot and was bleeding to death, it would cost me a toll and all that extra time to connect up with somebody to give me a hand."

It made sense for the indefatigable lady to move after all. But someone should have ensured that the house be kept as it was, when she went. Particularly the cosy, aromatic kitchen.

Nell had done us really proud. The big black kettle was singing away on the old iron range when we got to that room. In the centre a square, scrubbed wooden table was laid for tea. It was literally covered with plates of scones. All kinds of scones. All shapes. The whole room should have been lifted up as it was, including the dresser with its cups on their hooks, and kept in some place for posterity. A natural history museum perhaps. Neither the unforgettable smells of home-baking or the sights of a real wooden kitchen can ever be replaced. Children of the future will never know these wonderful experiences. They will have to make do with the coldness of chrome, the sterility of plastic and odourless cooking by microwave. God have mercy on their souls.

In the kitchen, Nell was even more fun. That's when she ripped off the jokes. She told me this one as I sat down to tea and scones, with butter, cream and home-made strawberry jam. I filmed the scene for the programme. Here's the story.

"There was a woman going in for a Highlander milk

contest, you see. She had to write a rhyme. Well she had got as far as 'Highlander milk when it's in the can, is the best milk in the land...' Well, just then, her husband came rushing in for his tea, because he had to go back to work. So she put her entry up on the mantlepiece and forgot about it.

Three weeks later, there was a knock on the door.

"Are you Mrs Smith?" A man in a suit was standing there.

"Yes," the woman answered.

"Congratulations, you've won the Highlander contest."

"Oh, no, not me, she said. "I never even sent it in."

Just then from behind her, her little boy piped up: "Oh, I sent it in Mum."

"But," said his mother, still disbelieving the whole thing, "I hadn't finished it."

"Oh," said the boy, "I finished it."

"Well," she said, "whatever did you put?"

"Well," he said, "you had 'Highlander milk when it's in the can is the best milk in the land'. So I just put: 'no tits to pull, no hay to pitch, just bash a hole in the son of a bitch!"

Nellie Fellowes sold her house and land, but not her gold claim, in 1979 when she was eighty-two. I spoke to her not long after she'd moved into her new home in Whitianga. She even had colour television, yet! At the time, she was settling in nicely thanks, planting a few citrus trees for the future. Sadly, though she'd had to bury an old friend before she left her home in Blackwater. The loner of Waiuta, Dick Willan had died in his bed. So I never got to film him. But I came awfully close one time.

Ovey Nelson: scrubcutter-poet from Kaikoura. *(photo by Don Grady)*

Filming on the West Coast for One Man's View. Director Hanafi Hayes and cinematographer Hamdani Milas.

Nellie Fellowes with the author on the porch of her Post Office/house, Blackwater, West Coast.

Carl Nillson, loner of North Cape.

Brawn and brains combine to solve a sticky problem. Unit manager Brian Walden and the author *en route* to Carl Nillson's. North Cane.

Brian presents the evening meal for inspection by Carl and Hanafi.

Crows-nest on Moturekareka. Snowy Harris and Hanafi aloft.

Setting out from Moturekareka with Snowy Harris.

With Oscar Coberger at Temple Basin Skifield, Arthur's Pass.

Hanafi (suitably padded) with Bert Sparrow and partner on ice.

Mrs Butcher instructs the author in the finer points of croquet.

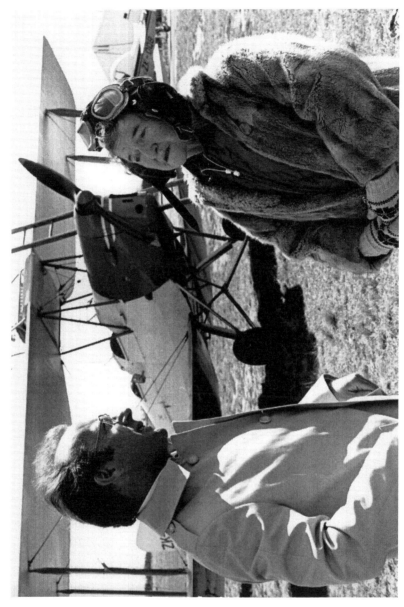

With Hilda Alexander, the Flying Grandmother.

Strapped in and terrified, the author prepares for take-off.

With Tim Vos, near Corbyvale, West Coast.

Waiting for the light to change. Tim Vos, Hanafi Hayes and cinematographer Hamdani Milas.

The Vos family, 1977. From left, Daniel, Kester, Tala (seated), Tim, Joella, Jos with baby Joab, Joachem and Reuben.

CHAPTER SIX

Loners

ONE OF THE KEY elements that contributes to the success of any television documentary is the research. This fact was particularly relevant in the case of a series of programmes I produced under the title of "One Man's View".

The filmed documentaries set out specifically to present a look at the unusual and the idiosyncratic in New Zealand. Both people and places.

To come up with places or situations that are guaranteed to be humorous or entertaining when translated to film is never easy. To find people who represent something different from the mainstream, who can be projected as "characters" to the viewer, is even harder.

I knew before I started seriously planning the series that a fair bit of the content would arise spontaneously. At least I hoped it would. Because it is usually the unexpected that provides the freshest and most exciting moments on film. Nevertheless, with six programmes with thirty or forty minutes to fill, I couldn't rely too heavily on that aspect.

First then, we needed someone who would scour each location for prospective material. I needed a researcher. Someone with a good sense of humour, the ability to track down, or uncover the unusual and with the personal charm to put people at their ease. The person would also need to have a fair bit of pluck.

A few people applied for the job. I chose the one with the least television research experience of the lot. I told her I was even prepared to overlook the fact that she had a Masters Degree for Arts. She had all I needed, without that. Spirit, a lovely laugh, a curiosity and a sharp intelligence. Her name was Jan Crocker, and she was a twenty six-year-old former teacher and world traveller from Christchurch.

Her first assignment would have thrown many right away. I sent her to the West Coast with the vague brief I've just mentioned: find me some weird and wonderful people and things that will evoke the true nature of that area. Well, one of the weird and wonderful people she travelled to interview, was the famous recluse of Waiuta, Mr Dick Willan.

The fact that she visited him on her own told me two things. One, that the five feet nothing Jan Crocker had spunk, and two, that she'd been lucky. He was stone sober when she met him. Had he been drunk, a state not uncommon to the man, I might have had the little lady's resignation the following day. However, she took a chance and that's what makes the difference between a good journalist and a mediocre one. And Dick had seen them all.

"Waiuta Dick" was pretty well a legend on the Coast. He lived in what was once the tiny police station, when Waiuta was a prosperous gold town. In its heyday, the town had a population of more than 800. Even as recently as 1951, 150 people lived in the remote spot. And its mine was still producing around 800 ounces of gold a month. Then the ventilation shaft caved in. Ever since, what was reputed to be the deepest shaft in the southern hemisphere has been full of "black damp", a highly dangerous gas. The mine was abandoned. Everyone left. Except sixty-nine year-old Dick and his dog. The guardians of a ghost town.

However, his reputation wasn't entirely based on the fact that he was a loner. Although that was what had roused my interest in the man. No, he was also the possessor of one of the blackest tempers around. When he was drunk that is. Indeed, he'd been banned from most of the hotels in the district in his time. Usually for fighting. And what he didn't hit with his fists, he rent asunder with his language.

It must have been a frightening sight to see him in full fury. The man from Waiuta stood a good six feet four inches tall, with hands like Primo Carnera and feet like a beat constable. Such havoc had he caused with his weakness for sherry, that the local policeman had prescribed that he be supplied with no more than two bottles per week. The publicans, no doubt happy to comply with anything that would keep the man away, kept to their bargain. Unfortunately though, over the years, Dick gained many friends and acquaintances who brought him grog. It was sad in a way. Sober, he was the most charming, gentle person you could meet. Intelligent, full of information about the old town and beauty of the country it sat in and courteous to everyone. He was a Jekyll and Hyde. I don't know whether I should consider it a privilege or not, but I experienced a taste of both sides of his character for myself.

I first met Dick after getting instructions from Nellie in Blackwater. They were easy enough to follow. Just keep going along the road. They're the kind of directions I like to hear. Waiuta was no distance at all from the little township of ten. Just round a few bends, heavy with bush, and then a steady climb to a plateau. It was up quite high really. In fact if the light was right and there wasn't too much smoke belching up from Greymouth's chimneys, you could see right down the island to Mount Cook.

Naturally enough, in the seventies, there were still many signs of the old Waiuta left. Each side of the road concrete foundations and brick chimney stacks defied time and the bush. They stood out from the long wild grass and encroaching gorse like giant gravestones. The wood walls had gone of course. Probably on Dick Willan's fire.

There was certainly a great deal of smoke coming from the rusty tin chimney when we arrived. The dog, as always, was first out to greet us. Not far behind and with a cheery wave of welcome, was his owner.

It was the same for everyone. Dick loved visitors. Mainly because he knew they'd be bringing the "plonk". But also because he genuinely liked to show them around his town.

Actually, you could hardly avoid meeting him, even if you wanted to. The road took you right past the former police station before leading to the old mine workings and the one time town centre. If you tried to drive past, Dick's sentinel dog would probably stand his ground in the centre of the road defying you. But most likely, you'd see the "postmaster" of Waiuta filling in potholes in the road. Well he didn't want his visitors to have too bumpy a ride when they came a' calling. The bottles may have broken.

Besides, it wasn't just friends that came to see him in those days. Many tourists had discovered the old ghost town, still reputed to be full of gold. Inevitably they also discovered Dick.

The title of postmaster he'd given himself. It carried no salary or responsibilities. Any mail for that citizen came up with his provisions and his sherry ration via Blackwater, once a week. But there was a telephone in one of the old buildings still in service. Since Dick was the only one who used it, he reckoned he deserved an official nomenclature.

He was also the unofficial mayor of the place. Because to be accurate, he wasn't always the sole resident. At holiday time one or two families moved in to baches at the back of the town. There was a massive concrete swimming pool left over for them to enjoy. Dick kept a fatherly eye on that too.

Our first meeting was conviviality itself. The big man, with a soft bushman's hat atop of his black bushy eyebrows and long sallow face ushered us onto his property. He showed us his vege garden and introduced us formally to his dog and the mouse on his wee porch. Then we went inside his hut for a chat in his "lounge". He was noticeably pleased to see that my unit manager hadn't forgotten the customary brown paper bag with two bottles in it.

He was proud of his home. The old office for living in and the former cell for sleeping in. Not that it looked like a police station when I saw it. Far from it. The bedroom, which couldn't have been much bigger than seven feet by five, had been freshly wallpapered. Very colourful floral designs graced its once sordid walls. An old friend of his had been up with the paper, the paste and of course two bottles of sherry. They'd made a good job of it, whatever the state they were in when they hung it.

The living quarters were to get the same treatment next, he told us. That's if they survived, I thought. Oh, the four walls surrounding his kitchen-cum-sitting room were hardy enough, but Dick had a worrying habit. Whenever the fire in his open hearth lost its flames and went dull on him, he just grabbed a can of kerosene and shot some on. The flames would leap practically across the room. It never seemed to bother him though. Or interrupt his flow.

He had a new lodger, he told us with obvious pleasure. Something, he didn't know what, lived in his roof. The old miner showed us how he communicated with it. It could have been an owl he suggested. Anyway whatever it was, it was an intelligent creature. And a friendly one. Dick banged at the ceiling with the end of a broomstick a couple of times. Sure enough, after a brief pause, his answer came. Precisely the same number of knocks were repeated from above.

Even so, Dick really loved to sit and talk with humans and he was a very companionable man to be with. The words came easily to the old bachelor. He'd been around. From the North Island originally, he'd sheared and scrub cut his way through the country until he turned to mining thirty-nine years before. When the mine closed down, he'd stayed on, picking up some gold here and there from the tailings. Latterly, of course, he'd augmented his income with the pension. He was doing all right too. No rent to pay and rates of about a dollar a year. He didn't need a huge income.

The big man's face would smile easily when he talked, his glass of sherry practically disappearing in the big hand holding it. Even though one of the fingers was missing. But then he was a seasoned performer, seen on television many times in his day and interviewed for books many more times than that. The only reason I considered including him in my programme was because he promised to reveal something about the mine and the town that had never been spoken of before. Even so, I was a little worried at the way his diction slurred after a couple of drinks. If we were to film him, I decided, we'd have to delay giving him any gifts until the job was done.

The decision was wise, but disastrous.

When we did return, Mr Hyde was in residence. A black, scowling face peered from the porch as we pulled up. Even the dog looked miserable. We didn't rate a bark. Dick Willan's only words of greeting were "Have you brought a bottle?"

I could sense that trouble was brewing, so I suggested my unit manager should pop in to see him first. To assess whether there was any point in staying around. Meanwhile, I wanted to show the camera crew some of the things I'd hoped to film around the mineshaft. Well, that's my story anyway.

My unit manager, a chap called Brian Walden, was quite a tough individual. He hadn't been back in New Zealand long after learning his trade in Hong Kong. It was true that Dick would have a reach advantage and about eight inches in height over him, but Brian was a sturdy lad. He had shoulders like a rugby prop and his nose hadn't been broken from playing tennis. It was a fair match on the whole.

We drove on leaving the unit manager on his way down the path to greet Mr Willan. Without a bottle. That was still in the camera van, along with the crew and me.

Our inspection of possible film locations was cursory. We knew there was really little chance of cooperation from Dick in his present state. At least when we returned to the outside of his house, we were facing in the right direction for a quick getaway.

As we approached, Dick's voice floated across the garden, loud and clear: "Have you got a bottle in there?"

"No," I yelled back, "we haven't." The effect was not unlike what happened when the man had thrown kerosene on his fire. He exploded with wrath, threatening all kinds of dreadful things. Including going for his axe. The abuse was both torrid and colourful. Part of me was hurt, another part fascinated. The mayor of Waiuta was infuriated. I wanted it on film, but the cameraman wouldn't leave the car. Brian Walden, my tough friend from Hong Kong was on his way from the scene fairly rapidly too, I noticed.

I was left with no choice. My cameraman wouldn't shoot film. My unit manager was opening the door and getting in the car and my subject matter was not exactly in the mood. Like the miners of Waiuta twenty-four years earlier, I had to abandon.

Actually, Dick ensured the retreat. His last words to me, still ring in my ears: "I wipe you, Hanafi Hayes, I wipe you!" We gave him a toot on the horn and left. It was a sad scene.

Now he's gone. Around Easter in 1979, they found him. On a Wednesday. Nellie Fellowes, down in Blackwater, told me she missed him terribly. She'd been talking to the Dr Jekyll part on the Monday, on the phone. He'd told her he would pick some laurel berries for her on the coming Thursday and send them down with the lady who delivered his provisions. But he never got to picking them.

And the Coast lost another character.

I met another loner on the West Coast, purely by chance.

He was different again. No wild-eyed recluse living in a ghost town with his memories, not this one. The very opposite in fact.

He was a travelling loner by the name of Norm Wardell. A retired gentleman of indeterminate age. Which means I forgot to ask him how old he was. I would guess that he was in his late sixties, though.

I spotted him first after I'd been filming the famous Kokatahi Band. We'd managed to gather that colourful collection of old timers together outside the Kokatahi general store. They played us a couple of numbers and had a chat on camera for the programme.

It was a rare occasion in a way. For one thing, the general store didn't exist any more. It was simply a house. For another thing, in 1975, none of the members of the band came from Kokatahi.

Anyway, we managed to find the old store sign from

someone's garage and stuck it up on the building. We also managed to persuade all the bandsmen to leave their jobs or their pubs for a couple of hours to be filmed.

They are a wonderful group of old characters themselves. Dressed in the traditional costume of the gold miner - red blouses, white pants with a gold stripe down the sides - they are a colourful sight to behold. Especially their instruments. They ranged from a violin with an old speaker horn on the top to a pair of bones that clackety-clacked out the rhythm.

I'd just been joking with these fellas about their strange instruments and their predilection for booze, when I saw him. Norm Wardell, I mean.

He was standing on the side of the road with some others watching the proceedings. A small man, with bright eyes and a smile on his face, he seemed to be literally loaded down with tape recorders and cameras. He was wearing a check trapper's hat with the ear muffs up at the side and a long gaberdine raincoat. He looked a little incongruous I suppose because it was a warm day and the sun was shining brilliantly. However, I don't think he could easily have taken his rain garb off if he'd wanted to. It seemed to be bound to his thick-set body by all the straps holding his equipment. But his overladen person had even more. Under one arm he had a pack of notebooks too.

Meanwhile, the bandsmen were denying all knowledge of the terrible lies I'd quoted to them about their drinking reputation. Then, when we'd finished filming, Norm moved in amongst them, taking notes.

I assumed that he was some kind of eccentric reporter for the local newspaper. After a couple of minutes, the musicians all made their way across the road to the hotel to make up some more lies and the old chap came over to me. He wanted to know what we were doing of course. But not for the local news. He was just interested in everything. So am I. Within seconds, I was the one asking the questions.

At that particular time, this walking research bureau was slowly making his way down the coast to Haast. On the way, he was taking pictures, making recordings and writing notes of anything that took his fancy. Not as a tourist though. It was a way of life. He told me he had cartons and cartons of material stored away. It was all either in Christchurch where he sometimes lived or in his van where he mostly lived. He pointed to it down the road. The vehicle, a minibus, was stuck in the mud on the soaking wet grass verge that bordered the asphalt.

He was a travellin' man. From time to time, that is. This time he'd been on the road for three months and his main aim was to gather information about the Haast Pass. Well that was his story. He said he was hoping to interview as many people as possible who were still "above ground" as he put it, who'd been associated with the making of it. He'd done the Otago side already, now he was heading south down the coast.

Right then though, he didn't stand much chance of getting beyond Kokatahi. The wheels of his van had dug in well and truly.

Now, I'm a reasonable man in situations like that. I offered the assistance of the crew to help push or pull him out. Provided he let me film him and his vehicle. He agreed.

It was all done very quickly, you understand. With no resistance on his part at all I might add. Indeed before we'd even got the camera up to him, he'd whipped up to his van, opened it up, reached inside and switched hats. This time he was wearing a pale fawn pith helmet. He saluted to signify he was ready.

I wasn't, though. First, I wanted to know where he got the hat. He bought it, he told me, for ten bob in 1962 in an auction room in Matamata, the dairy town in the Waikato. His philosophy was simple: if anything gives anybody a bit of fun, it's worth ten bob.

His van was certainly full of fun. It was simply stacked with all kinds of paraphernalia. For instance, in the cab, attached to the side of the passenger seat, was a large contraption with a propeller on it. A wind-driven generator, Norm informed me. For a six-volt battery. Then, in the back of the vehicle he had just about everything you'd normally find in a house, including the proverbial kitchen sink. It may not have been in any kind of conventional order, but it was all there all the same. Through the heaps of junk, I could see a fridge, table and chairs and a racing bike of all things.

A fascinating collection and a fascinating man. But rather a dark horse, I discovered. Not too interested to disclose too much about his life, apart from his quest down the Coast. He even covered up his number plate from the eye of the camera when we filmed. He slapped a handful of mud on it. But then, as Nell would have said, that was his privilege.

We all heaved to and pushed the van clear of the muddy verge and waved him on his way. The bit of film we'd shot on the run wasn't too great unfortunately, so it didn't make a place in the programme. After that, I didn't give the old chap another thought. However, he hadn't forgotten me.

Three years later, I was sitting out in my rumpus room working. I was struggling with a script for a documentary on Ostertagia. Oh, in case you don't know what that is, I'd better tell you. It's a small worm that likes to reside in the abomasum of a cow's stomach. That's not tripe, by the way.

As I was saying, I was hard at it ploughing through reams of research papers about this peculiar parasite, looking for a humorous angle. My rumpus room by the way, was a fairly large room at the bottom of the garden, with big french windows opening onto the lawn. It was a family room really, with wall bars, a dart board and a piano. Right then I was using it as a study. But it oscillated between being a play room, a bedroom for three of my girls and a quiet place for me to escape to and work. Sometimes it served all three purposes.

Now, I've always been a pretty private sort of person. Maybe as a form of protection, I've never bothered to publicise either my address or my phone number. Away from television, I always lived anonymously in a very ordinary house in a very ordinary suburb, in whatever city the period found me.

At this time, I couldn't even be reached through any television station. I had left the corporations and was working as an independent filmmaker with my own company. We had a clutch of rooms in Christchurch that few people knew of, but even so, I did most of my writing at my home.

I mention all this, so that you'll understand my sudden shock that afternoon. I looked up momentarily from Ostertagia to find Norm Wardell, my travellin' man from the Coast, standing at the open french windows of my rumpus room. So much for my privacy. He'd literally tracked me down. And he'd gone to a lot of trouble to do so.

It appears that he'd read somewhere that I'd formed a company in Christchurch called Telenion. So after making a number of enquiries in the area and coming up with nothing, he went to the Registry of Companies. From there he discovered the registered office. It happened to be my home address. So there he was. But why?

Well, it seems that the old itinerant researcher had other interests quite apart from gathering historical data. In the city, he belonged to a spiritualist church. He thought it might make the subject of a good documentary. Not only that, he said he knew a clairvoyant in Auckland, who in turn knew the identity of the murderer of Jennifer Beard. I believe that guy was also connected in some way, physically or metaphysically, with the spiritualist church Norm mentioned. All this unsolicited information was mine, gratis.

Now, as you may know, the murder of the young Australian hitchhiker was one of the great unsolved crimes of the South Island. You may also know that it's one that had drawn more red herrings than a rotten mackerel. It was a sad tale. Sadder perhaps because the case was never resolved and the crime's perpetrator still walks free. However, I must admit particularly at that time, it was not at the top of my list of things to worry about. I had quite enough problems trying to figure out how on earth I was going to make a twenty minute film about a worm. One that could only be seen under a microscope at that. As for filming the activities and experiences of a spiritualist church. Well, there was only one answer. Listen, look very busy, walk.

We had a fairly long back section in Christchurch. Nevertheless, slowly, with Norm at my side still talking, I walked quite purposefully to the gate. I said goodbye and wished him well, making a mental note to put the house on the market.

The end of the story? Well almost. Except that every now and then after that, I received little messages with strange symbols on them in the mail. From Norm of course. Most of them telling me where he could be contacted if I needed material for the film.

It's not hard to see sometimes why some people go to great lengths to cut themselves off from society. To get away from it all and be alone.

Not that anything would have induced me to go as far away from civilisation as one man I knew in New Zealand. His name was Carl Nillson and he lived alone at the top of the North Island. At a spot just south-west of North Cape.

The journey to get to this man's home was an adventure in itself. The last twenty-five miles had to be traversed by four-wheel-drive over wide, open, rugged terrain. I sent the fearless Jan Crocker ahead to scout. Her report a couple of days later was encouraging, just as long as the weather stayed fine. You see, about eighteen miles of the cross-country route was on a clay road. Need I say more.

Well, of course, by the time I was able to get there myself with a crew, the rain had come. And come. But we managed to get the park ranger to drive us there anyway.

Actually, Carl didn't consider himself a recluse or a hermit. He didn't like the terms. He hadn't cut himself off from society completely at all, he insisted. Even though he spent around ten months of the year living alone as New Zealand's northernmost man. The other two months, he was either visiting friends, or working on his son's farm at Waitaki Landing.

That was where the tough part of our journey started. After picking up Carl from his friends. The old chap had decided to come out for a while after the researchers had visited him. So we had to take him all the way back in again. Then for the sake of the programme, we would pretend we were meeting for the first time when he greeted me outside his house. Who says the camera never lies?

Anyway, Carl was staying with a Maori family just south of Waitaki Landing, so on our way up from Auckland by car, we stopped and met there.

He was a tall, thin, wiry man, with a day or two's growth of grey bristle on his chin and a lonely look in his slightly watery eyes. But he was hearty enough when he met us. Pleased we'd arrived and ready to accompany us back to his house on the coast.

It started raining again as we left for the ranger's house in Waitaki Landing, so the seventy-two-year-old loner added a woollen hat to his check shirt and heavy-twill trousered ensemble. The thin, twisted, roll-your-own cigarette in his mouth would no doubt defy any weather and stay alight. Whenever it dulled for a moment, the old man's cheeks worked away at it, sucking like a bellows.

Waitaki Landing is on the north-west bank of Parengarenga Harbour. It's also on the edge of the massive Te Paki Coastal Park. The crown land that stretches to Cape Reinga in the north-west and Hooper Point at the north-eastern tip of the arc of Spirits Bay.

Our journey would take us east and then north through this park, then east again through a massive tract of land farmed near Te Hapua. By then we'd be into some pretty steep country that had to be skirted. The next leg therefore would take us south first and then back north again over more crown land. Finally we would be on the raw and barren Waikuku Flats, a moorland of tea tree and wiri, defiantly growing out of the dead yellow clay. A few miles more, the paddocks would get greener and the Pacific Ocean nearer. And so would Carl's house, so he told us. In reality you would never know it. Surrounded by a cluster of kauri, pohutakawa and banana trees, it was camouflaged completely from view. Indeed you couldn't glimpse it until you got to within about twenty feet.

The only possible way to indicate to the viewer just how remote the spot was that Carl lived in, was to film the trek to it. Well parts of it anyway. I'd planned to shoot my progress across the various hazards, whilst driving with the ranger in his land rover. In the film I would be shown going to meet Carl at his home. So during all the initial filming, at times, the poor guy had to lie on the car floor, out of sight of the camera lens.

We knew from the researcher's report, that we had a creek to ford. It cut across the roadway and had pretty steep banks either side. Not a lot of laughs when the surrounding area was dry. However, as I mentioned, the rains had come and the water was bubbling along at a fair pace.

There was no cause for worry though, the ranger was prepared and equipped. He'd done the trip many many times, checking on old Carl throughout the winter months.

At the fording spot, he had it all worked out. Hop out of his vehicle, take his rope over to a specific tree on the far bank, back along to another tree and then to his winch on the front bumper. With me to assist, we were across in no time.

Actually my little show was just for the camera. Normally the ranger would do it by himself. It seems he used to tie the steering wheel, use the hand throttle, put it in low gear, hop out and pull on the rope. As it was, I hung on the rope and we filmed it to look as dramatic as possible.

Had I known what was ahead of us, I wouldn't have bothered. When we hit the clay road, we really got stuck. Up to our axles practically. And there was no simple routine of winching that could get us out of that. There wasn't a tree in sight. It was every man to the rope. Once again, I was lucky to have Brian Walden's shoulders along. He pulled like a mule to get us out. Carl helped too. He lightened the load by drinking a couple of the dozen beer he'd brought along for the ride.

Eventually, we made it and there, ahead of us, was the blue sea to the right, a massive pile of empty beer bottles to the left and the lush clump of trees that Carl had planted years ago, straight ahead.

We had planned to sleep overnight at the house, so the ranger now had to return through the clay, mud and slush and then come back to fetch us the next day. Meanwhile we made an early start with the filming.

"Good day." Carl and I were off, acting out our first meeting.

He was coming towards me from his house, I was just crossing the little wooden bridge over a creek that was escaping to the sea. "Good day to you, sir."

He was damn good I thought. Should have been in films.

As the name suggests, Carl Nillson was of Swedish stock. Well partly, anyway. His dad came to New Zealand from Sweden in 1868 and married an English girl at Wairoa. Carl was born in Palmerston North, but I don't think he hung around there too long. No longer than he had to, anyway.

At thirteen, he left school, calling it "humbug" and worked on his father's substantial land holding. Then at seventeen, he became his own master. His father gave him fifteen hundred pounds to buy some land of his own. Carl bought a farm at Dargaville.

But even as a gentleman landowner, he wasn't satisfied. So he headed north for the kauri gumfields, splitting his time between the two areas. His ambition and industry must have paid off. He ended up owning considerable areas of land in the far north.

Just before the Second World War, he got married and about the same time, he discovered the beautiful beach area of Waikuku now known everywhere outside of cartographers' offices as Carl's Beach.

A proud man, he sent his two sons and his two daughters to the best private schools that money could buy. Maybe because of his own shortcomings as a student. Then when his wife walked out on him, Carl turned most of his property over to his children and for ten months a year, opted out.

When I met him in 1975, he'd lived alone in his isolated house for nine years. It sat on a parcel of twenty-five acres leased to him for a peppercorn rent for the duration of his life or thirty years, whichever was the longer. All around him were signs that the man's zest for work hadn't flagged a bit.

He didn't need to work though. He still owned pockets of land here and there and he refused to collect his pension. His needs, he said, were small. Just beer, baccy and tucker. Oh, yes, batteries every so often for his well-used transistor.

On the paddocks, he ran a few cattle and sheep for company, and grazed his horse Jeff. He was the man's link with the nearest pub, if he fancied company any time. It was a thirty mile ride, but they took their time. It was often a good deal longer on the way home.

No, Carl certainly hadn't given up life, despite the pain in his eyes. Way out in the wilds, where a visitor was usually somebody lost, Mr Nillson's life was probably busier than most. He had his bread to bake, his fruit to bottle, his onions to pickle, his beer to brew, his veges to weed, his chickens to feed, his fishing and his beach to control.

That was Carl's most important job. Unpaid protector of Waikuku Beach. Indeed if it hadn't been for this one man's work, the beach may by now have stretched almost to Waitaki Landing.

Carl held it back. He planted lupins and marram grass. By the acre. In fact over the years, he'd established a hundred acres of grass on that rapidly shifting sand. Before he dies, I thought at the time, he will have planted a few more hundred acres. But they'll still officially call the place Waikuku Bay.

Carl didn't mind. If he did he would never show it. He was as deep as the sea he often just sat and watched. A man of great independence, he was also an expert in the one line answer.

"Was it because your marriage broke up that you came out here?" I asked him.

"No." he was emphatic. "I like it here. I always intended that I'd be here."

End of conversation. I couldn't help but admire his single-mindedness. But when I left him, I also couldn't help but feel a little sad.

No such feelings existed in me at the prospect of meeting the next loner we'd arranged to film. He was reputed to be a rascally old character. As much of a legend on the Hauraki Gulf as Waiuta Dick was on the West Coast.

His name was Clifford "Snowy" Harris, and for many years he'd squatted on the tiny island of Moturekareka. The thirty-nine acre lump of land is one of three small islands about four miles or so from Kawau, at the mouth of the Gulf.

The area is the boat-owners' playground and all the yachties and boaties knew old Snowy, if they didn't know "Clifford".

In 1975, when I first heard about him, Snowy was about seventy-one. In those days, he was still rowing himself across to the little store at Kawau to pick up his pension. Actually his business there was more of a money transfer transaction. He picked it up from the postmaster-storekeeper and gave it to the publican at the hotel.

At the end of the day, with a couple of cases of beer aboard, he would then row the four miles back home. On a few occasions, he'd been picked up drifting around the bays by the maritime ranger, but he was apparently a well-loved fellow and as he got older, some folk looked out for his welfare.

For instance, the storekeeper who issued the pension money, kept some back when Snowy raced across the road to the bar. With the money he'd salvaged, he made sure some food got put into the old chap's boat for the return journey. His favourite food then was Weetbix. He could soak and soften it with milk so that it slipped painlessly through his gums. Snowy had no teeth you see.

We stayed overnight on Kawau for the filming, travelling over to Moturekareka by launch. The weather was fine and the water so clear, you could almost see the beer cans covering the seabed. Sign that it had been another warm summer.

To get into the bay below Snowy's place of residence, we had to avoid the overturned hull of the shipwrecked *Rewa*. In 1926, the four-masted barque had been towed to the spot and sunk to serve as a breakwater. Unfortunately, the majestic old sailing ship had not gone to her grave willingly. She must have thrashed around a bit, because the wreck ended up a bit too far in to the shore for the best effect. Now her rusty bottom just basked in the sun.

Snowy was on the shallow beach waving to us as we approached, holding up a stick like a marooned Robinson Crusoe signalling for help. This chap didn't want to be rescued though. His enthusiastic greeting was intended to solicit more than goodwill. We were calling between pensions and there weren't many boats around in the gulf.

He was walking along the beach to meet me as I rowed ashore in a small dinghy from the launch. What a sight. His grizzled, wrinkled, old walnut for a face was half covered by an off-white beard. On his head he wore a woollen sailing hat with a little bob tassel, resting on the deep furrowed lines of his forehead. His clothes looked as if they'd been thrown at him rather than specifically put on. The old timer's frail-looking frame supported a big blue V-necked jersey and a pair of baggy old blue trousers, held together at the fly with a safety pin. But his feet must have been proud. They were sockless, and encased in a pair of good leather boots.

Snowy's brown eyes shone through the creases of skin as he smiled his toothless smile of welcome.

"Pleased to meet you captain. Welcome to New Zealand."

He stood leaning on his stick, his brown scrawny hand holding down a plastic bag round its top.

"What's that?" I asked, as I leapt out of the boat and pulled it onto the beach. "A rain-proof stick?"

His answer was an indecipherable mumble as he turned this way and that, looking for something I should have brought. "I've got a wonky ankle" is all I managed to catch.

"Well, how are you anyway?"

"Oh," he grinned, "still in the land of the living." By now, Snowy was aware that the scene was being filmed. However it soon became apparent that his heart wasn't in it at all. I suppose he thought we hadn't done the right thing by him.

As a nice, wee, spontaneous chat on the beach, the scene dropped onto the sand with a thud. All I could get from him was a few words about the *Rewa* and then the sulks set in.

He told us with some derision in his voice of the sinking of the *Rewa*. "She was a grand old ship. Used to be called the *Alice A Lee*. Oh, they just had to get rid of her and they brought her in for a breakwater, but she took charge of 'em." he chuckled. "They couldn't hold her you see with all that gear on her."

Over the years, Snowy had eased the load of the old ship in the bay. His little shack up the hill for instance, was formerly the old radio room.

A couple of minutes later, he left us and headed for it. I had hoped that Clifford Harris, who knew every bird and tree on the place would give us a conducted tour of his domain.

"Can we have a look around the island?" I suggested.

The sulks had started. "Nothing to stop you" he pouted. "Come on then." I started to move. Snowy wouldn't budge. Like a badly hurt child, he just stood there, picking at the sand with his stick.

"Can you show me around?" I tried again. "What's over here?" I pointed to a gap in the bush that fringed the beach. There was a path leading away somewhere. He wouldn't be moved though.

"You can find your way around. Got enough, now? Oh, cut it out," and off he stomped.

I certainly wasn't having a heck of a lot of luck with my loners, that's for sure. Snowy's behaviour was really surprising though. My researcher, Jan, had been over to see him and assured me that he'd be fantastic. She had come along on this trip too.

I looked at her then as we stood on the beach of

Moturekareka; my cameraman, my sound operator, my unit manager, Jan's fiancé who she'd squeezed into the party somehow and Jan.

She must have read my thoughts fairly quickly. "I'll go up and see him and try to persuade him to continue."

Jan took a couple of bottles of beer along with her to mix with the charm and she climbed the path through the bush up to his hut.

Just up from the beach, on a flat piece of land was another old house. Not a converted piece of the *Rewa* though. This was a regular wooden cottage and at the side of it was a well-laid out garden.

It was the original homestead. Apparently, Snowy had lived in it at one time or other. So too had the owner of the land. And although our old loner described himself as a squatter, his tenure was pretty secure. The owner had given him permission to stay on Moturekareka many years ago. Now everyone referred to it as Snowy's island.

I never did find out when Snowy first went there. I knew he hadn't been away for the past thirteen years. But before that he'd spent long periods elsewhere. At one time he'd lived for a while in Auckland building boats. Before that he'd been a merchant seaman. For four years he sailed on coastal scows, trading up and down New Zealand. Then he got a chance to go out into the deep water working the Pacific. All ports from New Zealand to Ocean Falls near Alaska.

The more I read over the research notes I had, the more frustrated I felt standing about waiting to see if he was going to play with us again. Then my researcher returned. With a smile on her face. She'd worked her charm apparently. He was having a rest, but he would come down in a minute. She'd told him how important it was, and left him with a glass of ale. We set up the camera for a chat with him sitting outside an old woodshed, just up from the beach. And waited.

Snowy was as good as his word. Within a few minutes, he came hobbling down the steep pathway from his hut. With his glass in one hand and the bottle in the other.

He was as cheery this time as he was glum when he'd left. It's amazing what a little affection and a transfusion will do for an injured sailor.

"Why did you decide to come and live on an island, Snowy?" We were back in the game again, with the camera running and the old chap squinting away into the sun.

"Well, I more or less got marooned here with me boat. I swapped boats with the joker that had the place and in the finish I finished up with nothing." He burst out laughing at that. "Not even the boat at all. A lot of fun, though." The glass found its way into a gap in the whiskers and the froth slid down into the toothless hole.

"I had five different bloody boats. Jokers wanted to buy them you know and like a fool you go and sell them, sorry about it afterwards. Lived aboard 'em for years..."

"You don't like living in town though?"

"Crowded... can't live with all the traffic. I've tried it. I can't rest. It goes day and night. Nerves, I've got nerves, man."

"Don't you miss the people?"

"Oh, I meet plenty of people out here now. Fishing boats, yachties..."

"But you prefer to live alone?"

"Oh, no, I don't, no. No, I'm glad of young people arriving out. I'm pleased about it. You get all kinds of visitors along there." He nodded towards the cottage by the beach. I knew that at the time there were two computer operators, of all people, opting out for a while. Living in the house. I believe the read-out on their savings had given them a year. Or until their parents found out.

"Young people having impromptu honeymoons and all that, you know," Snowy continued benevolently. "You don't say anything, you let 'em go."

"Do they invite you down for dinner sometimes?"

The old man emptied his glass again and gave a snort. "Don't think they can cook. Just live on love, I think."

"What do you do with yourself every day, then?"

"Oh, there's plenty to do. Firewood, cooking, pottering about, a bit of gardening." The routine was familiar. "Can't do what I used to now. I used to work like hell. Not now, me eyes play up on me."

He could still see what he wanted to, though, as I found out when he abruptly changed the subject.

"I'll tell you what happened one Sunday morning. A big flying cruiser job came in and I was crook after the grog as usual. And I sang out to them, 'any chance of a beer, please?' They said 'put your dinghy alongside'. So I rowed out and up came a bottle of champagne, half a bottle of sherry, a can of beer off the ice, food and clothing to the value of at least $40. 'Only stopping for lunch' they said. That was pretty good wasn't it? Must have struck them in a good mood, eh? End of the season, getting rid of their rubbish." Snowy chortled away.

"Let's go and have a look at your house, Snowy." I'd heard it was something to behold.

He led the way up the path, still talking. About the island now. "Got the best climate in the world. The odd tui." Then there was another bird noise he didn't know. "It goes all the time. First thing in the morning until last thing at night. Gets on the pohutakawa trees. I don't know what it is. I like the flax flower. Pity you couldn't catch the 'pukakis' floating around. There's about half a dozen of them. They're as tame as you like. They never stop squawking, though. They get on me G-strings a bit. As soon as anybody comes they soon disappear."

The way up to Snowy's hut was signposted all the way. Every few yards, a post stuck up out of the bush, with a yellow plastic container on top. In the dark, the plastic gave Snowy a course to steer when he made his return from the beach and his mates' hospitality. I'd heard though, that despite the flare path, he'd often stumbled off course and fallen down the home-made steps.

The old sailor's home measured about ten feet by eight feet.

Divided into two rooms somehow. The first impression you got, was that you'd entered an abandoned pig sty. One that someone had heaped all their rubbish into. The smell and dirt and staleness almost overpowered us. Nevertheless we all crushed in and started to set up the camera.

Inside the door, the first compartment held old rags hung from nails, shelves containing loo paper, tins of food and odd piles defying description. On the floor were heaps of papers and garbage. And a mousetrap. Snowy had mice from time to time. It wasn't surprising really. Except that he didn't just get the odd one. They came in swarms to share his little hut. He told me that at one time, he caught a hundred in a month with his mousetrap.

A row of small windows, grimy and cobwebbed, ran the length of one side of the building. Underneath, a wooden work top followed them from the first part of the hut to the main part. In there, we found Snowy's sleeping and living quarters. There was a bunk along one wall, covered in tatty, evil-looking blankets. Beside it stood an old stove, almost disappearing behind piles of ashes. At the side of the ashes, on filthy floor boards, a bent and blackened saucepan sat, full of stew. With grease and ash floating on top.

On the walls and low ceiling of this murky cabin, discoloured pictures of yachts, Marilyn Monroe and an astronaut decorated the scene.

The aged timbers of the *Rewa* had seen better days, I would say. And although the place was claimed to be borer free, I would think that just about every other form of parasite life in existence resided there.

Old Snowy didn't seem to mind. He offered the unit manager a glass of beer in the filthiest vessel I'd ever set eyes on. Then he settled himself down full-length on his bunk.

We'd set up to film there, with what little light we could produce. Snowy had other ideas though. He'd taken his woolly hat off and was scratching his bald head, getting ready for a sleep.

I told him I wanted to talk a wee bit about the domestic side of his life. He'd mellowed a lot since we arrived and again continued to cooperate. As long as he had his glass handy.

"Have you ever thought of getting married?" It was a stock question for old bachelors. Not that I expected to be as lucky with it this time as I was with Ovey Nelson.

"No. Oh, when I was young, I had a few love affairs."

"Did you?" This might be even better, after all. "Never had any money. I suppose I was lucky in a way." Snowy was lying down in his heap of rags, with his head resting in his hands.

"Why? What do you mean, lucky. You would have somebody to make your dinner wouldn't you?"

The old mariner wasn't impressed. "Oh, yeah, but what about the bloody arguments. Not many marriages are happy marriages, I know that much." He really meant it too.

I glanced down at the dreadful-looking mess in the saucepan. "What about your grub? Do you cook good food?"

"Oh, I'm not as fussy as I used to be. Cans, you get a bit sick of canned stuff. I cooked a pot full of vegetables this morning. Cut up some onions and I chucked a tin of bully beef in and that's what you call root t'goori." Now I knew. I thought it must be something exotic.

"Blimmen good feed. Not a bad mixture either. You cook up your vegetables, spuds, onion and carrot. Don't put any salt in because the bully beef's that salty. And mash it all and put the can of bully in. Makes a tasty feed."

I bet it does. No wonder he drank. No one in a sober state could have willingly dipped a spoon into that stagnant mess, sitting in the ashes.

However, since we had filmed it and had Snowy's beautifully explicit recipe, I felt I should make it known to the public. At the end of the programme, I superimposed the words: 'For the recipe for Root t'goori, write:' and I gave the address of the television station. I understand that not one person enquired further. The photography was excellent. It had captured all the horror that I'd seen in that greasy pot.

"What happens if you get sick?" The question was a natural

one to follow the food.

"Oh, trust me luck," said the old chap. "I take a bit of a risk, I suppose. A place like this, you don't really get sick. You get sick of being on your own ... "He was staring up at the blackened ceiling above his head. "They reckon there's no cure for loneliness. They reckon."

"What's your cure?" I asked him.

"Oh, I just put up with it. It doesn't matter now. I can't last much longer, can I?"

"Are you a religious man, Snowy?" I had a reason for asking the question. I was a little surprised at the answer.

"No, cripes, no. I don't go it at all. I've seen enough without bloody religion." The old loner settled his beard further down into his chest and switched his stare to the pin-ups on the wall. It was time for his siesta. I'd have to continue the conversation later if I wanted any more. I certainly did.

You see, I knew that Snowy had been involved in a tragedy at sea. He was the navigator on a yacht, mullet fishing off the east coast. The boat had gone down and Mr Harris was the sole survivor. After the incident, he retired from the sea and stuck to boat building or pottering around on Moturekareka. Some said he blamed himself for what happened. I wanted to ask him about it if l could.

The camera crew took a break for lunch whilst Snowy had his rest. But in the fresh air, away from the hut. And we weren't eating root t'goori I can assure you.

An hour or so later, our star was back and we had climbed up still higher to his favourite spot. Right at the top of the island, the old seafarer had built himself a lookout. It was in a beautiful setting too, on the edge of a plantation of pine trees that he'd grown from seed.

His crows-nest was made out of wood and corrugated iron. It was almost as big as his living quarters and sat atop poles and the branches of one of his massive pines. It must have been about fifteen feet above the ground.

Up the ladder and into the little hutch, Snowy almost bounded. This was his place of joy. In the summertime, he came up to spend hours looking around the gulf at all the activity. He was suddenly more animated than he'd been for every part of our visit so far.

"Good view in the clear weather. Coromandel straight across there about fifty mile," he pointed. "Waiheke, that's a haze. Bad sign. You can always see the end of the Great Barrier when it's clear." Snowy was in his element. Back on board again.

His leathery hand was showing me something else: "All kinds of boats floating around here in the summer. Good fishing just out there a bit."

"Boats have changed a bit now though, from your day, I suppose?" The conversation was turning my way, just right, I decided.

"Oh, crikey, yeah," answered Snowy.

"What do you think of all these posh boats with all the mod cons on?"

"Well, I suppose they're all right, but they don't seem to enjoy themselves like we did." He didn't need a drink now that he was really onto his subject. "I think half of them haven't paid for them, that's the trouble."

"Bit of mortgage problems you reckon?"

"They admit it. One joker comes over in his big flash boat and he says, 'what do you think?' 'Oh beaut.' And he says 'she's half mine and half the bank's.' He was honest, eh? She was a beauty too."

"You had a bit of a misfortune, didn't you, once?" I managed finally.

"On a yacht." Snowy quietened down a bit, but his eyes were still searching for something.

"Yes, were you wrecked?"

"Sole survivor out of four."

"Sole survivor?"

"I was blimmen lucky."

"What were you then. Skippering, or what?"

"No, I wasn't. The skipper was ah... he had the yachtmaster's certificates and he was that seasick, he nearly died."

"What happened then? Where was it?"

"Down Parongahau, just out of Napier."

I obviously wasn't going to get this story too easily. One line at a time the answers came. It was like pulling teeth. Not a very apt simile in the circumstances though.

"What happened?"

"Oh, it blew all our sails out and got caught in a stinker and blew ashore and two of them they never found and two of us got ashore and the other bloke died of exposure." Snowy got it all out in one sentence without stopping. He had no intention of elaborating unless he had to.

"How did you keep alive then?"

"Oh, I just kept going, something keeps you going. Just made it though." He allowed himself a pause to remember a moment of thirty years past. But only a brief pause. "I'd had a pretty good yachting season. I was pretty fit."

I'd got as much as I was going to get of the story that changed the man's life. Snowy was fidgeting again, so the serious stuff had to end.

"You're still pretty fit for your age, aren't you?"

"Oh," he gave his little chortle: "I don't know, me 'eart's not too good... especially after the grog. You get the odd palpitations."

"Will you row me to Kawau?"

"Oh, no, you make it too hard. It's getting too much for me."

"Alright, well take me around the corner... we'll just go for a row." I needed the shot for the end of the film. But Snowy was back in his stubborn mood once again.

"Oh, I had a row this morning... I rowed just on two miles..."

In the end, I had to settle for just having him in the boat. I had to row. But it was worth it for the closing line of the film.

The cameraman and sound operator were high up on the hill. I was in the boat wearing a radio microphone. The idea was to film the boat and its occupants fairly close up to start and then for the cameraman to zoom out and hold for the final shot.

"Hey, Snowy," I shouted across to my passenger, "what are you going to do with the rest of your life, eh? Where do you go from here?"

The old chap's face creased into a grin and his voice came back loud and clear: "Into me grave." End of the film.

But Snowy was proved wrong. He never made it into a grave. Not even into Davy Jones' locker, where he very nearly went when he was forty. Old Clifford "Snowy" Harris died just before Christmas in 1978. It seems he hadn't been well for some time.

The old legs were playing him up and he'd not been getting about too much around his beloved Moturekareka. Or in his dinghy. He hadn't been across for his pension in some time. Instead, some of his many friends had brought his groceries over to him. Either the fishermen, the ranger or boats from the Royal New Zealand Navy could be relied on. In fact a navy boat made a point of calling in regularly to check on him. On one of the checks, they, found him dead in his little radio room.

The locals in Kawau arranged for Snowy to be cremated in Auckland. Then they took his ashes back to his island and scattered them there. Amongst his friends - the tuis, the little white-eyes, the 'pukakis', the kingfishers, the magpies that sometimes visited him, the penguins and the seagulls that knew his secrets.

CHAPTER SEVEN

The "Old" Athletes

ONE OF THE HAPPIEST programmes I ever made was one that featured veteran athletes and sportspeople. I called it "Life Begins at Seventy".

It was enjoyable for several reasons.

Firstly, it was something of a revelation to me that so many of the so-called older generation not only participated, but excelled in sports in New Zealand.

I'd retired from playing soccer at the grand old age of forty-one. Well, my boots were worn out and I couldn't afford new ones. After that I had to content myself with jogging around the garden and jumping to conclusions. I'd assumed I was no different from anyone else in that respect. Oh, I know that some rugby players knock a few years off their official age and run out for the fight well into their forties. But judging from the pot bellies most New Zealand middle-aged males sport, I would imagine that the most exercised part of their anatomy is the elbow.

However, research for the programme on old athletes proved that the belly-bulging-over-the-belt was a comparatively new phenomenon in Godzone. There were still many lithe and active males around. Although they were nearly all in the autumn of their lives.

Another reason why the documentary was a pleasure to do, was simply because all the people in it were old. Not so much perhaps just because they were all accomplished old sports. But because they were old and mature people. You see it was becoming more and more evident that the very old and the very young provided me with the most entertaining material for programmes. They are the most relaxed and least inhibited.

After twelve a child is shy about his puberty, his spots and his speech. After twenty he is worried about his image. Then at forty, he just needs a drink.

The same applies to the female side too.

Old people, with the odd exception, have usually dropped their vanity, they care little about their image and they can talk more freely from experience. In short they say what they think in the way that they want to. They don't feel the need to measure up to any phoney expectations. That's what makes them great.

To a lesser extent, young children are the same. Natural. That's before society demands that they hide their innate personality and then moulds them into what I term "acceptable similar citizens". They are forced to do something drastic if they want to overcome this stifling cloak. Either call on the fallacious freer of constraint that you buy at the bar or just opt out of it all. Some have to do both.

I think it was no more than coincidence, but all the people I finally chose for the programme came from the South Island. Maybe there are fewer distractions there. Or maybe it was due to the fact that we were running low on the budget. I can't recall. Nevertheless, some of the "stars" of the film would have been difficult to match how ever far I'd cast my net.

Take eighty-five-year-old Larry Devlin for instance.

When I filmed him in 1975, he was not only regularly playing golf (with a handicap of fifteen by the way), but he put in a full week's work as an auctioneer and real estate agent. Indeed, when I spoke to him four years later, he was still at the helm of his firm in Rangiora.

But then Larry was extraordinary. Not only was he an active and skilled golfer by any standards, but he was a one-armed player. Not by choice, let me hasten to say. No, he'd apparently lost his left arm in a machine accident when he was a lad of thirteen.

Heaven only knows what his sporting life would have been like if he'd had the use of both arms. As it is, he was also a skilled billiards player. He once beat the New Zealand champion Cedarberg in 1919 without realising who the guy was he'd been playing. An astonished marker informed him of the fact after the game was over and the balls back in the pocket.

When I met this old athlete, I just couldn't believe his age was correct. He looked at least twenty years younger. The man was tall, upright, bespectacled and had a full head of dark brown and silver hair. His mind was alert, his manner forthright and he had a warm and gentle sense of humour.

We met, naturally enough, on the golf course. Though he would have been equally at home on a tennis court. That's right, Larry had also been a champion tennis player of some note in the south. He'd given up playing that game seriously when he was a boy of fifty-five. That's when he took up the game of golf.

Oh, yes, he'd also dabbled in bowls. Way back in 1920, would you believe. However he expressed his feelings for that game in this way: "It's so inactive that I couldn't be bothered with it. And now, when I get old... if I get old, I'll play bowls. But not while I can play this..." Whereupon he drove a powerful shot right down the centre of the fairway. The man, let me just remind you, was then eighty-five.

Who knows what his maker has lined up for Larry. No one can tell. However, if he is destined to stay around Rangiora for a few more years, I have no doubt he'll be playing a certain challenge match. A forty-five-year-old junior in Larry Devlin's local golf club had promised to play him on his hundredth birthday.

I wouldn't put money on who would win, either. Not if this amazing man still sticks to his Irish philosophy about the game: "When you're swinging, you want to start off at top speed and gradually get faster!"

The baby of my film, at seventy-three, had a similar attitude to life I suspect. Though he certainly wasn't Irish.

Oscar Coberger, the doyen of the New Zealand ski slopes, hailed from Bavaria. Actually a lot of people took him to be

Swiss before the Second World War. But then Oscar had to be interned. He must have missed the slopes quite a bit during that period of his life. They don't get a lot of snow on Somes Island or Pahiatua, where they stuck this intrepid athlete.

Fortunately, for the sport, the experience didn't dampen the man's enthusiasm one whit. If anything, it may have increased it. He certainly wasted little time subsequently. Apparently, this grandfather on skis was always around at opening day of the season wherever the field was. And they tell me he would usually still be skiing on the last remnants of snow at Christmas time.

Oscar was a giant of a man and even in his seventies, as hard as granite. I still remember with discomfort, following him up to a ski field on foot. My little legs were aching as I stumbled behind his relentless, seemingly effortless, pace up the track to Temple Basin, high above Arthur's Pass.

"Chust kip a steady pace, not too much in a hurry and not too slow," was his advice as we climbed the hillside. He looked like a mythical guide into the unknown. His battered leather snow hat wrapped around his ears, his gaunt face set and unsmiling and his great arched nose pointing the way. I believe he even carried my bag on his shoulder along with his skis.

We were going to some lengths, and heights, to film the athlete in his natural environment. Whatever the cost. To me I mean. Well normally, I suppose, as a so-called television personality, I should have been a bit more circumspect. I'm sure many others would have. As it was, on this particular clip, I would look absurd. The visual comparison was most unkind.

There we were: one a lean, lithe, courageous young athlete of seventy-three; the other a short, stumpy, leaden footed witness. One searing down the snow-packed slopes of a massive mountain. The other, dressed in a borrowed woman's ski jacket, with a ludicrous woollen hat flopped on my head, looking like a teapot waiting to be poured. I'm not mentioning the fact that my nose was blue from the bitter cold. Or that I was young enough to be the other's son.

But then Oscar was the hero and who could deny it as he leapt into the air past the camera. Mind you, he considered the kind of thing he was doing for television child's play. Just slipping down the gentle slopes wasn't what had earned him his considerable reputation in New Zealand skiing circles.

He wasn't happy about the light either. And although he didn't actually say so, I got the distinct feeling that Mr Coberger would probably have preferred to direct the sequence himself. He was a very single-minded old skier, let me tell you.

His real forte though, was what he called mountaineering skiing. Not just going up and down, like softies. But to ski around and over the top of mountains. That was his preference. In fact this student from Stuttgart introduced the technique of alpine skiing to New Zealand as long ago as 1928. And when he talked about going around and over the mountains, he really meant the mountains. Mt Cook for instance, the majestic and challenging pride of the Two Thumb range, just at the back of the Hermitage.

Oscar didn't actually ski over the top of Cook, but he holds the senior record for ski climbing at 10,000 feet on that little peak. He also holds another record. He's the oldest person at that location, to fall 400 feet in an avalanche and survive. But then he was only seventy-two when he had that little adventure.

Nevertheless, the incident upset him. Not the physical discomfort from any injuries he sustained, oh, no. The skier was annoyed rather than hurt. Annoyed that he'd lost his mouth organ and his "Sherlock Holmes" hat in the fall. They were in his pack which lies entombed in the snow to this day. He wasn't too happy with the Accident Compensation Commission either. Apparently they rejected his claim for assistance to redress his suffering. They said that he didn't qualify because he was self-employed.

Mr Coberger couldn't complain too much though. He

enjoyed most of what he wanted out of life, including a good deal of respect. He had an alpine goods shop in Christchurch and a mountainside chalet/shop in Arthur's Pass, where he was reputed to be the self-appointed mayor. Certainly the local newspapers and politicians hear regularly from him on the needs of the district. As far as they affect skiing anyway.

To Oscar, his sport was the crown of sports and embraced his three ideals: exercise, risk and culture. He demonstrated all three for us in our final shot. He'd bought a new mouth organ, so after we said goodbye, he skied off playing a slightly squeaky rendition of a Dvorak symphony...

Had he heard the music, I'm sure another oldie I met and filmed would have danced to it. On his ice skates.

Bert Sparrow, a seventy-eight year-old retired builder, was the Christchurch Fred Astaire of the ice rink. He may well still be. If not he'll be water skiing, another of his passions when I knew him.

The man was remarkable in many ways. He was so enthusiastic about everything he did. Physically, he was a neat man. Not too tall, not too thin and not too much hair on top. But he liked the ladies. In the most fatherly or grandfatherly way of course. Actually, when he was still gliding the light fantastic on ice with a twenty-year-old beauty in his arms, he was in fact a great-grandfather twice over. That didn't slow him down though.

His favourite dance was the Alexandra Tango, one of the most technically difficult dances for skaters to tackle. In terms of class or category of competence, it represents gold. And many young champions gained their success with old Bert as their partner. One girl became the Canterbury Junior Champion when she was fourteen and her partner, Mr Sparrow, was sixty-eight.

Bert the builder had been widowed since as long ago as 1940 and although he never remarried, he never gave up living either. He was, he claimed, the first bloke in Canterbury to go water skiing. That was when he was a mere forty-three. Had we filmed this dapper senior citizen in the summertime instead of winter, we would have been able to show him hurtling across the water on skis. At seventy-eight, remember.

I never did take up his offer to join him in his boat, to experience that particular thrill, but I did join him on the ice.

Now, I have no sense of balance at all. I get extremely worried if I'm flying and the plane goes over to one side. So trying to stay upright on skates is a major feat for me. Not so Bert. Mind you, he did give me a lot of encouragement and hope. He didn't start skating until he was forty-five and it was a further nine years before he turned to the really clever stuff of dancing on ice. Gliding along to music on two thin strips of steel. By that time, it seems, his interest in the sporting life was interfering with his business. Bert considered it was the other way round, so he retired. Well, there was the golf, the snow skiing and the billiards to think of too, you see.

But it was the ice dancing that he enjoyed most of all. And it was that which attracted my interest for the film. Throughout the programme, with each of the participants, I'd endeavoured to share something of their particular talent by joining in. A game of golf with Larry Devlin, a frozen foot with young Oscar and so on. This one I knew was going to be the most difficult for me. How on earth could I interview Bert while we danced a waltz round the rink together? Well you know how people tend to jump to the wrong conclusions. Especially since the old chap would have to hold me up and close all the while. No, that was out. But I had to try to talk to the man whilst he was skating. The only answer was to get someone else along and let the two of them hold me up between them. So we did. A twenty-three-year-old blonde. Well you might as well enjoy the work.

I still managed to look preposterous. Wedged in between the two, supported at the forearms like an undernourished invalid. My costume didn't do a heck of a lot for me either. Bert had managed to rustle up someone's discarded ice hockey gear from somewhere. Oh, it was reasonably innocuous from the front, but the back gave me the appearance of a circus clown towards the end of his act. I don't know what position in a team the owner of the outfit would have played in a game, but this little number sported a great hunk of padding on the seat of the pants. Very practical I thought, when I first donned the uniform, especially for me. I knew I'd be spending a fair amount of time on that part of my anatomy, how ever many people I had to support me.

It proved to be of no value to me at all though. The person who'd discarded it had good reason to. The darn padding was unstitched and hanging loose inside the seat. It dropped. At times I felt it down behind my lower calves. And my good friend Hamdani, the cameraman, kept insisting on shooting the three of us from behind.

I managed the interview however and Bert was very patient with me. Well you try answering questions when the person who is asking them keeps collapsing and grabbing at your legs.

Fortunately my old sportsman still had good strong legs. He told me he did twelve knee bends every night before he got into bed. I had a job even bending the sheets back before I got into bed after that session.

But there was not time to indulge myself with stiffness and bruises. I had to put all that behind me. Well I had done at the time really. You see we were filming on a very tight schedule. I think I'd allowed myself about eight days to shoot the entire programme that included seven or more locations. Some of them many miles from our base. Even so, I needed to be careful, I wasn't getting any younger myself.

My next athlete, although an expert in a much less aggressive sport, put me to shame. She was old enough to be my grandmother. And she was still playing.

Her game was croquet, she was then eighty-eight and her name was Monica, Mrs Monica Butcher, a sprightly and very active widow who lived on her own in a big house in

Cashmere, a rather "naice" part of Christchurch.

This sweet old soul had been playing her game in competitions and championships for sixty-eight years, would you believe. Starting on her parents private green at the family home in Amberley, she'd never been far from a place to play. Indeed in Cashmere, she couldn't have been much closer. The local club's green was just the other side of a little wooden gate in her back section hedge. Whenever anyone vaguely resembling a croquet player ventured on to that surface, Monica would reach for her mallet. For a game of course.

When we called round to film, I didn't know a croquet mallet from a tent peg mallet. Let alone what you had to do with all the hoops stuck in the ground. But once again, I had a patient instructor. Monica dressed for the occasion too. White dress, white cardigan, white shoes and a little white straw hat atop of her white hair. She endeavoured to explain the game to me.

"No," she affirmed in answer to my enquiry, "it's not just a matter of belting the balls through the hoops with the mallet. There's much more to it than that." She studied the green through her rimless glasses, pointed to the balls and explained: "Now of course, blue and black are partners and red and yellow are partners."

"Of course," I said. I hadn't the vaguest idea why. Rules of games are a complete mystery to me. Immediately someone, anyone, tries to explain systems or instructions to anything, my mind goes blank. It takes me weeks to pick up card games although I can forget how to play them in hours. I just don't seem to have the mental equipment to ingest detail. Or the patience.

I'm more of an instinctive performer, if you like. If I see a big wooden hammer, some fair sized balls and some hoops stuck in the ground, then I tend to want to swing the stick and belt them. If there is a specific or designated place for them to go, so much the better. But if not, I'm just as happy, simply knocking them all around the park.

The game of croquet isn't like that at all, of course. I mean, you can't imagine the Queen swinging her mallet around wildly, laying about her on the greens of Buckingham Palace, can you? For one thing, there'd be the danger of her bringing down one of the corgis or one of the many horses that roam around the place. Philip might even be tempted to retaliate with a charge and lunge with his polo stick.

"No, croquet is a very scientific game," Mrs Butcher went on. "Now, first you make the hoop... the idea is to place your balls so that you can make as many hoops as possible in one turn."

That sounded absolutely frightening. Much worse than falling on your behind on the ice rink. At least I only went one way on those occasions.

For the sake of the film, I concentrated as hard as I could on the incredible instructions that this sweet little old lady was giving me.

"Could you give me an idea of how I should start off with my first shot?" Now that was a very simple, unloaded, sensible question, right?

Just in case you aren't familiar with the game of croquet, let me set the scene. We were standing at the outer perimeter of a flat piece of closely mown grass, measuring about thirty yards by thirty. Maybe thirty yards by forty-one, now that I think of it. There was a slight breeze coming from the south-west. This was having no effect on the game, but was playing havoc with my hair. Around us was the characteristic sound of the city of Christchurch. A gentle snoring.

Mrs Monica Butcher, white as a ghost, was crouching slightly with a mallet clenched firmly in pale, bony, freckled hands. She surveyed the "green", the patch of grass I described a moment ago, her eyes focussing on the first of six hoops or loops of metal, like giant fencing staples, that were stuck into the ground at random spots.

I was also bent slightly forward, holding a long wooden-handled mallet between my outstretched legs. On the ground, in front of the club end of my mallet, was a ball. The camera was running, I was in position, tense and hoping to hit the first stroke successfully to its obvious goal, the little hoop about five yards away.

Then Monica answered my question. "Well, now, the first shot you play over to the side-line. You don't attempt to make your hoop."

So there I was, my mallet poised ready to carry that ball straight to the hoop. My eye had practically worn a line in the grass. Then the lady said "No". I was completely psyched up for nothing.

"Why is that?" I asked, shattered.

"Well, because you haven't a hope. You take your mallet in from this line. You have to try to make your hoop from there. If you fail, your opponent can hit the ball and make a hoop and go on."

"Oh, I see." I didn't have the faintest idea what it was she was explaining. My fault, not hers.

It didn't get any easier, either. My first shot, I was told, was a roquet shot, my second a croquet shot. By the time we got to my third shot, I decided to call it a day.

I'd leave that game to the English aristocracy and the wonderful octogenarians of New Zealand.

I was lucky that my next assignment for the film required me to engage in a sport I have no trouble with at all. Swimming. Also the people I'd arranged to film were all much nearer to my own age. Well a bit nearer.

I had an appointment with the swimming grandmothers of St Albans. A jollier group of ladies would be hard to find. Five or six doughty ladies who swim all the year round and all but one of whom were into their seventies.

We met on neutral ground at the massive Olympic size pool at Queen Elizabeth Park.

The aqua-girls were all in the water when we arrived and I got a bit concerned for them after a while. You see, the natural light in the building wasn't sufficient for filming. We had to rig a lot of artificial lights. Anyway, by the time the lights were up and the cameraman had taken umpteen light readings, the girls were looking a bit goose-pimpled and blue. I had to do something to make sure they didn't go sour on me. So when the cameraman was finally ready, the meeting started with a splash. I jumped in on top of them.

But they were great sports every one of them. More than that, though, they would prove a great stimulant for any viewers who had never swum and had regretted never learning. Many of these belles of the baths had taken the plunge very late in their lives.

For instance, a rather substantial bundle with the distinguished name of Rene Kirk, hadn't learnt to swim until she was sixty-eight. Even then she started in an unorthodox way. The first stroke she mastered, was the backstroke and for three years that was her only stroke. I don't know whether she dived in backwards to get started, but it was always on her back that Rene could be seen in the waters of Christchurch. Flailing up and down. Then in 1971, for the first time, she put her face under. From then on she could see where she was going. At seventy-four she was crawling like Johnny Weismuller.

Once again, there was a tremendous zest for life amongst these folk. Diving off the metre board, practising life-saving or performing their water ballet. That's right. It may have been true that none of them looked remotely like Esther Williams, but for the camera, they floated into position like lilies in a duck pond. Long may they all stay afloat.

It's sometimes said that some New Zealanders are more British than the British. I'm not absolutely sure who it is that sometimes says it. Maybe the American tourists who have discovered that Britain is no longer like Britain. At least like the Britain they were sold at the travel agents.

However, it's equally true to say that there are plenty of Kiwis who have a different view. A few even profess little affection or desire for affiliation with the island James Cook sailed from, more than two hundred years ago. Some denied their ancestry when Britain joined the European community, others when they couldn't get a work permit over there.

Nevertheless, there are still some, whose roots were planted here several generations ago, who remain steadfast in their loyalty to the mother country.

One such person was another of the remarkable athletes that I featured in the film "Life begins at Seventy".

Les Arnst was seventy-four when I first met him. At that time he was the oldest competitive cyclist in the world. In fact not long after I filmed this wizard on wheels, he rode in the classic Christchurch to Timaru 100 mile road race.

It was an event that brought him great personal satisfaction too, no doubt.

Way back in 1921, when he was a youth of twenty, Les had competed in the same race and won honour for being the fastest junior. His time then was 6 hours and 32 minutes. In 1975, when he was just two months short of his seventy-fifth birthday, he did the journey again. This time in 5 hours and 20 minutes!

Certainly the road surfaces had improved since then, even in the South Island. But it was still a marvellous achievement. Indeed Les was an unusual man. Let me tell you his theory on things British.

First you have to understand that Les Arnst was a Hanoverian. A supporter of the English Royal House of Hanover. He was a religious man. An Anglican churchman who believed that the British are descendants of Isaac and the Queen is a direct descendant of David. Not only that. Les was of the definite opinion that the Union Jack derives its name from the biblical name, Jacob.

So, this tall, thin son of Canterbury, with iron grey crew-cut hair, gold glasses and the unmistakeable soft, South Island speech was: "British to the core and proud of the Queen", to use his own words. And that's after two generations of living amongst the culture of rugby, racing and beer. His grandfather came to New Zealand in 1874 and Les insisted that Hanoverians are of different stock altogether from

Germans. The ones, presumably that come from Hanover. If you follow.

Anyway, Hanoverian, German, British or Hungarian, he was a fine athlete. And a healthy one. Apparently, he hadn't been to a doctor in forty years, he kept himself so fit. Part of the reason, obviously, was his cycling. He claimed it was his medicine in fact. But his diet also played a big part he said. For one thing, his wife used to make him "bike riders' bread" which was a kind of fruit loaf.

That was a luxury item though, judging by what he normally had for breakfast: a carrot and an apple. The only drink he would take was dandelion tea and rarely, a glass of beer. For lunch, he'd go mad and wade into a salad. Then off he'd pedal, on another training spin. Even in his mid-seventies, Les cycled around the Christchurch suburbs every day. Totalling between two and three hundred miles a week.

I asked him if he'd ever done any jogging, as it had become such a popular pastime for the over-fifties. Oh, no, he'd said, he was too lazy to jog. He'd rather cycle a hundred miles than jog around the block. It was ironic really. He was fortunate that not too many shared his passion for keeping his feet off the ground. When he was in business that is. You see, Les was a retired foot specialist.

The last person to appear in this scenario for super-annuitants certainly kept her feet off the ground. At least she did when she was performing her thing. Indeed when the camera first picked her up for the opening sequence of her bit in the film, she was 800 feet above the ground. Standing on the wing of an aeroplane.

Hilda Alexander, who didn't know that I knew she was seventy-eight at the time, was the oldest woman ever to fly in this fashion in the world. She still is, I believe.

Incidentally, this was one episode where I really did dread having to participate in the same manner as the "old expert". But when it came to it, I had no choice. Dear Hilda challenged me before we actually started filming.

"If I can do it at my age, then so can you... if you're man enough."

Let me explain exactly what she meant. She was inviting me to stand, just as she did, upright, on top, outside that is, on the wing of a Tiger Moth single-engine biplane. While it was in the air.

Now, I'm not really a coward. I mean, I was prepared to risk my life trying to stand vertically on ice skates. I have, in my time walked across rope bridges over deep gullies. Well ten feet deep. I've even walked unaccompanied down Queen Street in Auckland after dark. On late shopping nights. But stand on the wing of a plane?

At that time, I had a phobia about even flying inside of one. It's true. I was the archetypal "fear of flying" passenger. Every time I boarded one of those unnatural vehicles, it was like the first time for me. The thought uppermost in my mind was not so much will it crash, as when will it crash?

Maybe I would have been happier if I'd studied aerodynamics. As it was, my mind was always full of terror. Every noise was a warning of impending disaster. Every movement of the craft, a sign of dreadful trouble. And there was no way that I would either look out of a window or leave my seat during a flight. However long it took. I wouldn't even unbuckle my safety belt when the little illuminated sign came on with a "ding". In truth, I always assumed the "ding" was another passenger in strife, calling for a stewardess. As for getting up and going to the toilet at the rear of the plane, there just was no chance of that. I would rather sit in kidney-bursting agony than risk being in that compartment when it fell away from the rest of the aircraft. Hard to believe that I was once in the RAF isn't it?

Thank goodness, I've since conquered the problem. Simply by having to fly to so many places. However, at the time we were filming Hilda Alexander, that, quite truthfully, was my state of mind on the subject of flying.

But what could I do? This fantastic great-grandmother had thrown down the gauntlet. I had to pick it up. All I could hope for was that I might pass out as we took off so that I would know nothing about it. Meanwhile we had to film the little troublemaker.

Mrs Alexander was a wee ball of a woman, especially in her flying rig. Gingery frizzy hair escaped here and there from under her leather helmet and she wore a great big fur coat on backwards to keep out the cold. She was a feminine person for all her antics in the air. For the camera she'd managed a touch of rouge here and a touch of lipstick there and her shiny brown eyes showed she enjoyed a good joke.

First we filmed her way up and over the Cathedral in the centre of Christchurch. That was done with the cameraman shooting from another light plane a few feet away. When they all got through that dice with death, I talked to her down on the ground.

Why on earth, to use a singularly inappropriate phrase, did she do it? Well in the first place, because her son had done it. She actually didn't take up this sport or madness, call it what you will, until she was seventy-three. I never found out what she did for kicks before that date. Bullfighting on ice I shouldn't wonder.

The spirit of thrill-seeking was certainly in the family. Even her grandchildren had been up there, she told me. That was another reason for my soon-to-happen act of bravado. They were all there watching us.

It had all started though, as Hilda said, with her son, Ron. He was the first man to fly across Cook Strait on the wing of a plane. Now they've got ferry boats of course. Usually though Ron performed at the controls. Indeed he was one of New Zealand's best-known aerobatic flyers. Over the previous five years, Mum and son had appeared with the act at pageants and air shows all over the place. Ron in the cockpit and Hilda standing outside alone, waving her hankie to the crowds from upwards of 500 feet. And if that wasn't enough, this incredible lady specially requested her son to tilt the plane from time to time. She got bored just following a steady course.

However, she was still human. When I asked her if anything unusual had ever happened whilst she was up there, she answered: "Well, no, not so far. I wouldn't like anything unusual to happen."

My sentiments entirely, I thought, when my turn came.

The little climb up the ladder was like mounting the platform for the guillotine. Madame Lafarge Alexander was standing at the side knitting and grinning away below me. Actually just getting onto the wing was enough for me. Already I was a good ten feet off the ground. But once I was up there, I couldn't turn back. They'd taken the ladder away, and started up the engine.

In the centre of the plane, an upright stand was bolted into the top of the wing. It was set at a slight angle and served as a back rest, supported by a pole each side. The idea was to stand against this and be harnessed to it with safety belts across the chest. Once I was strapped in, I pulled my goggles down, tried to control my legs from shaking violently and gave a weak smile to the camera below. We were off.

At first, I couldn't believe what was happening. Had I really agreed to this? Was this really me standing on top of a Tiger Moth with a whirring lethal propeller a yard or less from my feet? What would happen if I fell? If the harness were to snap and I fell forward onto the blade?

They say that just before you die, you see your whole life in rapid playback form in a matter of seconds. Well I didn't exactly experience that. But I did manage to conjure up just about every permutation of horror that could possibly happen to me in that situation. And we weren't off the ground yet. Maybe Ron won't actually take off.

That was my next thought. Perhaps he'll have realised how absolutely terrified I really was. Sure, he could just fake it for the camera and then pull up at the end of the runway and turn around. He didn't though. We were off the ground. My God. Yes, that's right, that's all I could think of, My God. Please save me.

If ever you're having a problem with your belief in a

Creator, any doubts at all as to where you naturally turn when faced with certain death, then fly on the wing of a plane. I prayed incessantly. Over trees, over fields, over buildings. The whole of north Christchurch has been prayed over. And then we were back on the ground. My faith was intact. My prayers had been answered.

All the same, I wouldn't be doing that again. Challenge or no challenge, that was for sure. Hilda Alexander was more than welcome to that particular thrill.

As things turned out, though, the little flying great-grandmother never went up on the wing again. I found that out some time later, in 1977.

I happened to bump into her in a small coffee shop in Riccarton. The old dare-devil didn't recognise me at first, but then she came over. She'd aged slightly I noticed, but was still full of fight at eighty-odd. She wanted me to do her a favour. Would I write to an address she gave me, to verify that she had flown on the Tiger Moth wing, on the day that we filmed. Apparently the information was being sent off for entry in the Guinness Book of Records. Her name would be recorded officially at last as the oldest lady to fly on the wing of a plane.

Unfortunately, her son Ron, who started it all, would never see it recorded in print. A few months earlier, he'd lost his life in a crash at an air show in the North Island. The plane he was piloting went out of control.

CHAPTER EIGHT

In Search of Gracious Living

IN THE SUMMER OF 1976, I finally managed to paint the roof of my house. That meant that I only had two more outside walls, the rumpus room, the garage and the entire inside of the place to do. I started the work in 1974. As things turned out, in fact, I didn't complete even the outside until the autumn of 1978. In the meantime, the house certainly had a distinctive appearance. Half of it was an insipid peach tone, with blue trim and the other half was cedar brown with white trim. By the time I did manage to get back to it, of course, I had to redo the walls and window frames I'd accomplished four years earlier.

The trouble was lack of time. Because despite the success of the documentary series "One Man's View" and my rapidly advancing old age, I found myself having to work harder than ever to make films.

Thanks to the terrific encouragement I received from TV2 at the end of 1975, I decided it was time to start my own independent film company. It was a wish I'd been nurturing for quite a few years. Actually it wasn't my company. I was one of four directors on the board. We were also the work force. It was the only possible way I could envisage such a venture being tolerably viable. Especially since we were starting from scratch.

None of the four had any money. We had to invite investment and loans from friends and relatives to buy all the costly equipment required. The simple incentive for the work force was if we succeeded we got paid. If we failed we didn't. It was going to be a new experience anyway. In public service broadcasting, it usually works the other way round.

We called the company Telenion Productions Ltd. We got the name from the gate of an orchard in Heathcote, a

Christchurch suburb. Our first offices were a ten dollar-a-week suite in the old University of Canterbury buildings. It had been evacuated as a scholastic institution and converted into an arts centre.

Space, in this ambitious project, was available at cheap rates for people or organisations engaged in cultural, non-profit-making pursuits. I had a heck of a time convincing the manager that we qualified. Well no one ever believed that television was in any way connected with culture for a start. Also how could a private film company claim to be non-profit-making?

Well of course, it took no time at all to establish our ability to become a non-profit-making organisation. The man's trust in us was not unwarranted. The figures in our first balance sheet justified all. As to the question of culture, that was taken care of when one of our directors volunteered to sell flags for the arts centre fund-raising day.

Our three small rooms were furnished with desks and chairs that had been left, stored or abandoned by the former students or staff of those hallowed halls. We managed to paint out most of the obscenities, fortunately. The block that they were situated in had some fascinating tenants. Most of the other occupants purported to advise or guide the disturbed.

Below us we had one or two drug and alcohol prevention agencies. Next door we had a Scottish lady parapsychologist and next to her a transcendental meditation school. They were all right, it was the neighbour up above us that annoyed me a bit. He was a landscape designer and he had access to the roof. In fact he had a little flower bower up there. Well, that's quite fine of course. I'm all for flower-bower power. Unfortunately he bestowed as much care and attention on his flowers as our other neighbours did on their customers. He must have been watering all the time. Eventually, the water seeped through our ceiling. So in our main room, our front office, we had first damp, then crumbling plaster and finally a large patch of unplastered bare laths.

Consequently we had to make sure that any potential clients never looked up.

It really was a most pleasant location though. Until the music students arrived after four o'clock that is. Then the air all around would be rent by the earnest efforts of would-be Menuhins, callously sawing away at their instruments. Much of the space was taken over by the Canterbury School of Music, you see. Too much. I would think we had the pre-destined rejects struggling away in another of the rooms below our suite. Unless it was a therapy session for demented alcoholics.

However, for most of the time, it was very congenial there. Especially when the surly boilerman turned up in time to get the heating going. But then who cares about heat when they're setting out on a new adventure.

Only two of us had previously had any film experience. Myself and the cameraman, Hamdani Milas, a young Aucklander. Nevertheless, with our expectations high and our budgets ridiculously low, we walked the tightrope of independent filmmaking together. It didn't take me very long to appreciate the truth of Ovey Nelson's comment on self-employment either. Remember? "The hardest boss you can work for is your bloody self, if you ask me." He should have tried working on commission for "the broadcasting".

Behind me for ever, though, were the many years of working for the NZBC, plus possibly the most difficult year of my life, working on contract to TV2. Well it was never more than TV1 and a 1/2 in my day, actually. Their coverage was so sparse.

When the old corporation was split in three by the Labour Party's Roger Douglas, the new executives all started off in good style. They all went off on their overseas "study" trips for starters. The trouble was that they didn't learn a heck of a lot from them. Except how to adopt ideas that are in practice in other countries. If you do venture outside the shores of Godzone, you'll find out very soon just where all the names and styles of programmes on New Zealand's screens come from. On the other hand, you don't tend to find a lot of plagiarism of Kiwi style television programmes in say, the UK or the US. Raratonga? Maybe.

It's true that there were a lot of rumours that Sir Kenneth Clark had modelled his series, "A Place in the Country" on a series I produced called "Open House". But flattering as the thought was, I have to deny that there's any truth in it. It was simply a matter of coincidence.

In fact, he hadn't seen my programmes and I hadn't seen any of his. The only point of comparison that existed between the two sets of documentaries was the budgets. My total budget for six fifteen-minute films, would just about have paid his cameraman's salary for a year. Whereas, the budget for one of his programmes would have paid all my company's salaries and covered all costs for me to produce the six programmes I did called "Open House".

At the time, I was grateful that TV1 was interested in buying them at any price. Indeed that corporation gave Telenion just the lift-off it needed. Not only did it commission the series on old New Zealand mansions, but it gave us first payments on two other documentary ideas I'd submitted. Our first year of operation then was virtually underwritten. Provided we cut every possible corner imaginable and kept our costs to the minimum. Hence the ten dollar offices. And a misguided decision not to employ a trained researcher.

I think if the trusty Jan Crocker had been around, I might have tried to rustle up the money somehow to employ her talents. However, by that time, that little lady had got herself married and moved to her husband's home in South Africa. In the circumstances, there was no such thing as a freelance television researcher. Anybody with either the inclination or the aptitude for such a job was already employed by one or other of the broadcasting corporations.

I would have to do the job myself, I thought. It would mean a heck of a lot of extra work of course, but I figured as things were, I could do a lot worse. It transpired that I not only could, but I did. Do a lot worse, I mean.

How it happened, I just can't remember. But somehow, through a friend of someone who had a friend who knew of someone who's hobby was old houses, I met this chap.

He was a tall, long, dank fair-haired youth of nineteen. His principal interest was studying music at Canterbury University. In fact, from what I gathered, he was quite a talented bloke, able to compose symphonies with fewer problems than I have frying eggs. However, it was his interest in houses and any knowledge he had of very large ones that caused me to meet him.

I suppose I should have taken note of my initial impression of the lad, when he turned up in a long black Dracula cape. But I very much hoped he would be of help. I even overlooked his rather high English-sounding voice.

The fact is, this budding Chopin from Palmerston North knew about houses. At least he told me he did. He had a great wad of photographs of them and pads and pads of notes that he'd taken during the course of his investigations. He told me he was accumulating all that data to write a book. His writing would establish how the wealth and landowning in New Zealand was in the hands of people who all shared the same ancestor or two. No not Adam and Eve. He meant a couple of the early settlers in the country.

His studies usually took the form of sitting in front rooms, having tea with knowledgeable and talkative old ladies. That way, he was compiling his dossier. The lowdown on the loaded.

He had a great deal of confidence, I must say. I think he'd been a student at Wanganui Collegiate, judging by his obvious *savoir-faire*. I decided he might well be the researcher I needed. I offered him the job for a couple of weeks, searching and following up leads in the North Island. All expenses paid and a light fee. Plus a rental car at his disposal. He accepted, even agreeing to my suggestion that he leave his black cape behind in Christchurch.

The mission was little short of a disaster. His penchant for chatting over tea and bickies or even gin and tonics may well have been most enjoyable. However, when a week or so had passed without a word from him, I got a bit concerned. I flew to a spot near Hastings to meet him and get his report.

I had discovered that he was staying with an old school chum in the district. That's where I had to go to pick him up. Up to that point, he'd visited his brother in Wellington and his family in Palmerston North, but he was pretty certain we could film in a house at Masterton. All the other contacts I'd given him had turned him down flat.

I wasn't sure how many other relatives he had scattered over the North Island, but I couldn't take a chance. For the remainder of the second week, I had to take over. With this sensitive, but callow boy a fellow traveller. A miserable one at that. If the journey to a prospective house meant driving over loose metal roading and it often did, he groaned in his seat like a seasick drunk.

After visiting a few places around Hawkes Bay and the Wairarapa, I told him I wouldn't need his services any longer. When I left Palmerston North on a flight for Auckland, I left alone. It had been a fairly short business association, and I'm not sure now whether he was hurt or not when I terminated it.

However, I was hurt, extremely hurt and darned annoyed when I discovered that the few notes of research that he had accomplished were riddled with inaccuracies. Inevitably, I ended up doing all the research for the first three houses. Luckily, my wife volunteered to do the remainder.

My episode with the erstwhile musician-researcher, had been a time-wasting and costly interlude that I could well have done without. Imagine if you can then my reaction to a phone call I received some time later. My friend with the cape was calling to tell me that he insisted on a credit in the programme for research. If he didn't get it, he threatened, he'd sue me. I told him where to go and it was a good deal warmer spot than Palmerston North.

Actually, the idea of the documentaries about old mansions came to me when I was looking at the possibility of doing a programme on New Zealand's landed gentry. My aim incidentally wasn't to unveil some incestuous New Zealand plot to control the nation's wealth. It was simply to see and show how those who had it, used and enjoyed it. Anyway as things turned out my proposal didn't get off the ground. But it had introduced me to a book of drawings and notes on some North Island homesteads. The author was an architect called Michael Fowler, who later became the mayor of Wellington.

The book had opened up a whole new world to me. A world of the past. One that not only illustrated something of New Zealand's heritage, but also titivated my curiosity about the lifestyle of the wealthy. At first it was difficult to believe that such huge places existed. I was naive enough to think that outside of Karori, Remuera and Fendalton, New Zealand was an egalitarian society. That all the rest of us lived in 1200 square feet wood frame houses and drove old bangers to work.

Certainly I had a sneaking suspicion that some of the constantly whingeing farmers may have had another car in the garage. Left over from the "good times" of course. But I had no idea that a few still lived like lords of the manor. Not in Kiwi land. I was obviously wrong.

Some of the houses I later found, were nearer to ten thousand square feet in size. And there are a lot of them dotted all over the country.

However, for various reasons, many of the owners didn't want us filming them or their houses. One reason I could understand. The master of a forty-roomed mansion in the South Island, for instance, was worried about potential burglary. He felt that exposure on television might invite less friendly inquiry later. Apparently it was impossible to lock up and guard his rambling home. Therefore he sought anonymity if possible. Fair enough.

Some of the other excuses were a little less acceptable, I felt.

A fascinating and very grand home in South Canterbury for

example couldn't be included in the programme because it was owned by an absentee landlord. That was the reason given. The house was extremely old and belonged to one of the two most influential farming families in the South Island. The families that originally burned off and settled thousands of acres of land for sheep farming. Well the third-generation owners of the estate didn't live on the property. They also had another big estate further down the island in Southland. Meanwhile, the house that I fancied, was a virtual museum, tended by a housekeeper and her husband. The vast farm was in the hands of a manager.

I was a bit annoyed at the owner's reluctance in this case, for several reasons. I knew for a fact that the house was steeped in history and fascinating stories. I also knew that one of the *objets d'art* it contained was the organ that Samuel Butler played when he was in the district. However the hardest pill for me to swallow was the knowledge that the current owner was a terrific eccentric. A real character I was told. But I didn't even get to meet her.

Two other places of great interest and size that I was attracted by had to be excluded for pecuniary reasons. Both the wealthy owners wanted to be paid. One of them had just returned to New Zealand after winter holidaying in Fiji. I thought that was a bit rude.

Then there was the Riddiford estate at Pencarrow. I had known about that gem many years before and forgotten about it. When I was planning my series I realised that the mansion on that property would be ideal. It was old. It was lavish and its design was quite unusual from what I could remember of it. Apart from that, I heard that it contained a ballroom, about the size of Lancaster Park, which often still rang to the strains of the waltz.

Now all the flavour of grandeur may seem incongruous, when you realise where Pencarrow is. In fact, I suppose most people associate that name with the sewer outfall pipe. The passage that carries the capital's effluent clear of the harbour and into the open sea. Southerlies permitting, of course.

To get to the property required an hour or more drive around the coast, often over loose metal roads. I understand it was considered the country residence of one branch of the Riddiford family. The owners also had a flat in town.

I knew of it because I once had to track down a group of distinguished international seismologists. They were in that area studying rocks and earth for possible earthquake data. The famous Mr Richter was amongst them. I was hoping to get a brief interview with one of the party for a news programme in Wellington.

Anyway, when the camera crew and I reached the place where the group was supposed to be working or consulting or whatever distinguished international seismologists do together, we couldn't find them. So we continued on and by trespassing through a series of gates, we found the house.

It was like something out of a Hollywood movie of the thirties. In front of it was a large swimming pool, reflecting the grand glass pavilion style architecture of the building.

I went up the wide steps tentatively and rang the bell. I expected a white-haired black butler to answer my call at least. But no, it was a glamorous lady in a long dress, with fair hair resting on her shoulders. She had a small wine glass in one hand I recall. The lady of the house, I presumed. It was all very romantic.

Her accent was as English as my lady from Karori. She informed me that the party I sought had been guests at the house for lunch. They were now, she waved her hand with the glass in it, somewhere over there.

I eventually found the group and then made a fatal mistake. Instead of playing safe and interviewing Richter on the day's finding, I decided, quite arbitrarily, to ignore him and go for someone else. The man, whose scale is quoted every time there's a shake anywhere in the world, had had too much coverage already, I reasoned. He may have been the world's number one authority on the subject, but I wanted to give someone else a chance. I opted for authority number two, a Japanese gentleman. I should have played safe.

The little interview took place by a cluster of rocks on the craggy seashore. My choice was both charming and well-informed. I'd done the right thing, I remember feeling at the time. Unfortunately, the interview proved disastrous.

The sound recordist must either have blanked out or else he hated me. The film was fine. The Japanese chap looked good. However, it was impossible to understand a word he said. Not only was his accent extremely thick when reproduced on tape, but the sea was in tumult. The seagulls came across beautifully though. We had to can the whole thing. Still I had seen that unusual house.

So, many years later, the Riddiford property was high on the list for the series. But it wasn't to be. When enquiries were made for permission to film, we were turned down. It was a great disappointment, because it meant I wouldn't have an example to film in the Wellington district. Already another Riddiford had turned me down across the hills in Carterton. I was beginning to think the family had something against me.

Not that everything was plain sailing in Auckland, either. The first house there, I fancied, declined to be included. It was a lovely place, tucked away in affluent Epsom. The owner felt our presence might disturb the family.

The second, the biggest stone house in the nation, was the Pah, in Mount Roskill. The owners of this mammoth place were quite willing and their reception most friendly, but this time, I had to withdraw. You see for some time, the house had been a residence for nuns in training.

At least there was Alberton, the big white mansion in Mount Albert with its incongruous Indian towers and girdles of balconies. The house was then a museum, the property of the Historic Places Trust. Because of that it posed a few problems.

You see, my hope in making the programmes was that with each property, I could present something of its past existence and the lifestyle of its present occupants. In most cases, I knew there was a link between the two. That many of the homes would still be in the family. And that the present generation would have stories that they'd had handed down to them.

Alberton's link had been severed. The last member of the family to have lived there had died and left the old mansion to the nation. Much of the information that existed about the place had been compiled by interested scholars. Some of it was speculation. Some derived from distant relatives.

I was a bit dubious as to whether I could make an informative and, importantly, an entertaining, programme about the house in Mount Albert. I was also aware that as a museum, it had been featured on film before and that knowledge never excites me. The only justification then for making a programme about Alberton would be if I could find a completely new angle. I struck gold.

About two or three weeks before I made my initial enquiry, it appears that an old lady had turned up at the house. Her name was Mrs Marjorie Amoretti, a widowed lady in her early eighties.

Apparently, she had paid her entrance fee, just like all the other visitors, and made her way around, from room to room. But she was no stranger to the place. That soon became obvious by her comments and questions. She informed the curator that some of the furniture placings were wrong, for a start. The man asked her how she knew. That's when my angle revealed itself. Mrs Marjorie Amoretti had lived and worked in the house as a servant girl. That was when she was fifteen year old red-headed Marjorie Marchbanks.

When I heard the story, I knew I had a film.

If the old lady was still active enough and willing, she could take me and the viewer on a conducted tour. Better still, I was hoping she'd be able to recreate for us something of the life that existed there. As seen through the eyes of a young maidservant. I arranged to meet her as soon as I could.

She lived no more than a couple of miles from the place we were going to film, in a neat-as-a-sandwich State house. Ironically, before her visit of a few weeks earlier she hadn't been near Alberton for more than sixty years, I learned.

Some people grow old gracefully, some age well before their time, but Marjorie Amoretti was ageless. She could have been anything between sixty-five and seventy-five in appearance, but her spirit and mental attitude were as bright as a twenty-year-old's.

She was a slim lady with brown alert eyes, a resolute chin and still a touch of red in her hair. If I remember correctly at our first meeting, she had a pair of black slacks on with a top that hung loosely outside of them. Not a typical great-grandmother, I felt. But a proud one. Pictures of her family, all generations of it, were well represented in her spotlessly clean home. Marjorie had done the wallpapering and painting herself, of course.

Her memory, I discovered, was as crisp as the white net curtains at her window and she would be more than happy to oblige with the filming. In fact she became so interested and enthusiastic that I had to ask her to hold on until we got in front of the camera. I wanted this lady as spontaneous as possible.

So, instead of telling me about the family, the gatherings in the ballroom or the bustle of the kitchen, Marjorie showed me just how fit she herself was. I couldn't believe it. I don't know, to this day, how we got on the subject, but this eighty-two year old lady was challenging me to touch my toes. She could do it, with ease. She demonstrated her talent and then demanded that I try. I couldn't. Not without tearing all the tissue in my spine and bending my knees up to my chin.

Well of course, I was doing it all wrong. I then got instruction on how to lift my torso up and out of my pelvic casing and then throw it down towards my toes. The old tutor made it look so easy and she wouldn't relent until I conquered this improbable gymnastic contortion.

The scene was absurd. I'd merely gone to do some research. To see if the old thing would look and sound all right on camera. To make sure her dentures wouldn't click when she spoke and to find out if I could prise something from her long forgotten past.

Instead, I'd ended up in the lounge of a wiry, ruthless fitness instructor, old enough to be my grandmother, struggling to touch my toes. I got there, eventually, I had to, otherwise she'd never let me go.

I said goodbye and walked away from her house about five inches taller than I'd arrived. It took about two weeks for my torso to fall back into the pelvis.

I certainly didn't have to worry about that little old lady, unless she insisted on jogging around the house for the film. But when the time came to do the filming, in fact she did give me a bit of a scare. The crew and I moved up to Auckland and into a motel the day before we were due to start. I had some last minute research and planning to complete. That's when I discovered that Mrs Amoretti had suffered a bad bout of influenza.

I phoned her to make sure she was over the illness and still prepared to turn up at 8 o'clock the next morning. I got no answer. I tried a couple of hours later, but still the phone just rang and rang.

Now, as I've mentioned before, I am a supreme pessimist. My mind always conjures up the worst. The old lady lived alone. She wasn't answering the phone. Three things only were possible. She was too ill to leave her bed. She had been taken to hospital. Or, dread the thought, she had died and was lying undiscovered in her lounge. Possibly in the middle of touching her toes. My film would be ruined. Someone would have to go to her house to check. The unit manager.

It would be baptism by fire for the poor guy. This was his first experience of what is called "an unexpected contingency".

In New Zealand terms, in those days, a unit manager was a person of many roles from clapper boy to accommodation arranger, to lugger of equipment, to driver, to the one who had to look after "unexpected contingencies".

The chap who now occupied this distinguished and onerous position, had never been involved in filming before in his life. He was a friend of mine. His background had included a bit of teaching, a bit of accountancy, owning a bread round and possessing a cheery disposition and strong arms. He had all the attributes expected of a unit manager under normal circumstances. Now, we'd find out how he would shape up to an unexpected contingency. None too confidently, he left the motel and drove to her house.

I waited, expecting the worst. Trying to figure out whether I should continue with Alberton as one of the programmes, or whether to abandon.

An hour later, the unit manager returned to the motel. I searched his face as he got out of the car, looking for justification for the despair I felt. But he was smiling. All was well. Indeed, our dear Marjorie was still very much with us, he told me. It seems that she didn't hear the phone ring, simply because she was out in her garden pulling potatoes.

During the next couple of days, this wonderful old lady was a joy to be with. Not only as a mine of information, but because her attitude was so patient and cooperative. I don't think she actually sat down throughout the whole period. Unless it was when she relented and accepted the offer of a cup of tea.

Everything was "no trouble at all". At times, she had to wait around for long periods while lighting was arranged or filming was halted for some reason or other. We had power cuts, visitors walking through and the odd *contretemps* amongst the members of the fledgling company. Throughout it all, she just smiled her gentle smile of understanding.

The lady had lived a lot. And worked a lot. Starting for about a shilling a week in the backstairs of the hundred and eleven-year-old Alberton. The house was less than fifty years old when she was there of course.

She went up the stairs like a fifteen-year-old to show us her former bedroom in the attic. It was a tiny cell with a sloped ceiling and a window at one end. She sat on her old bed and told us how she used to creep to the top of the stairs to peep when the parties were held down below.

We walked along the yards and yards of verandahs that

she'd scrubbed on her knees and we wandered through rooms she'd not been officially allowed to enter as a maid.

Finally, when we were sitting in the big ballroom, I asked Marjorie if she would have liked to own a house like Alberton. Her answer provided a neat ending to the film when she said: "No, not a bit, it's too cold for me. Would you?"

I didn't give her my answer, but if I had, it would have been yes. I love big old houses. I'm very much attracted to the atmosphere that usually exists in them.

That's why I was anxious to move on to our next location a wonderful old mansion called Matapiro. It was in the lovely rolling country of Hawkes Bay, a few miles away from Hastings.

I was also anxious to move on for more practical reasons. The more time we spent on the road filming, the higher the costs would soar. On this first project as an independent, there was no spare fat. Motel accommodation had to be cut down to the minimum. Not just the number of nights, but the number of rooms too. The director-workers in this little enterprise would really get to know each other by the end of the series. Wherever we could we had to cut corners. If it normally took four days to film a programme, we would have to do it in three. We had set ourselves a schedule with all that in mind.

We weren't able to keep up with it of course. You never can.

In our case, the plan fell apart after completing the first house. On the morning of our departure from Auckland for Hastings, the sound operator felt violently sick. He kept throwing up.

At first we thought it was something he ate. We'd been to a suburban pizzeria the night before and he'd been eating the stuff like it was his last meal on earth. It practically was. When he came back from the washroom at the airport, he looked like death. He staggered up to us with the news that he was retching up blood.

At that point, it was obvious that we couldn't pop off and film Matapiro. The man was hardly able to stand. So we booked him onto a flight to Christchurch and ordered him to see a doctor. He never filmed with us again. His story was sad indeed.

His name was Peter Hastings. I'd met him scarcely four months earlier. When he came into my orbit of acquaintances, I didn't even know him as a sound operator. I knew only that the sensitive forty-year-old bachelor was a brilliant classical guitarist, considered one of New Zealand's top three exponents of that instrument. I didn't know then either that he'd also played violin in the Sydney Symphony Orchestra. He was something of a mystery in fact. A shy man, bald and bearded, he lived alone in Christchurch and made his living as a proofreader for the *Christchurch Star*.

It was only when we were toying with the problems of forming a film company, that his other talents became known.

We needed a sound operator. Not just that, though. We needed someone who could do the job for as little reward as possible. Initially at least. But not only that. We wanted someone who would also actually put some money into the venture.

Now there aren't too many people with those qualifications around. Peter was one, we discovered. Strange as it might seem, he'd been a sound technician with the old NZBC, when it was the NZBS. He was on the same training course he told me as a certain Kevan Moore. Not only that, Peter was working as a studio sound mixer in Australian television a few years ago, when the same Mr Moore was a studio sound boom operator on the same programmes. It's a small world isn't it? When Peter Hastings was just about to take up the earphones and tape recorder again, his old colleague Kevan Moore was the Controller of Programmes for TV2.

Anyway, the former violinist for the Sydney Symphony and one-time pilot in the RNZAF threw in his job as a proofreader and threw in his lot with the film company. For one film only.

When Peter returned to Christchurch, the rest of us, cameraman, unit manager and myself, took the time to visit the next location. To make our apologies and plan for when we could return. Then we went home to wait for the next step. The news wasn't good. Our sound man was initially prescribed nothing but rest. Later the doctors diagnosed cancer.

Once again we were faced with the task of finding the impossible. Once again, our man came from out of the blue. This time, a young chap who'd never touched a tape recorder before in his life presented himself. He was a friend of us all, who'd been interested in our project from its inception. His name was Hammond Peek and he was a drop-out from the design school of Canterbury University.

When I met him, he was courting the daughter of a friend of mine and selling his home-made jewellery to anyone who'd buy it. A big fellow, he hailed from Picton and was endowed with a natural ability for the practical. Indeed he was and still is a stickler for meticulous detail. A guy who'll never settle for second best. We were lucky to have him along. Particularly since he was prepared to work for little and stick his share in the pot to buy his directorship.

We had a week at the outside to train him for the job. We had re-arranged our schedule for our return to the North Island. Instead of shooting two houses up there in one week, we planned to do three. They were Matapiro, Akitio, a very grand homestead at the mouth of the Akitio river on the southern coast of Hawkes Bay and Brancepeth. The last one was a spectacular place just outside Masterton. In the meantime, search and research for houses in the South Island had to start to crystallise.

Mr Peek took to the sound business like public relations men take to broadcasting. With both hands. Within the period he had more than a rudimentary understanding of the job. It was just as well. Filming inside the old houses was a challenge to anyone. Mostly they were dark, which meant sticking up lights everywhere and restricting space. Usually, they were very high-ceilinged, which tended to bounce the sound around like an echo chamber. There was also the problem of movement.

I was always concerned that the subject might die on its feet, if I didn't keep things moving. Consequently, I tended to try to film as much as possible in a natural flow. Preparing at least two sequences in advance. That poses even more horrors for a crew. So our twenty-two-year-old trainee was going to have to learn his craft the hard way. Starting at the top.

Matapiro was a very attractive, gabled house with white and black panelling. It looked very English, sitting high at the top of a long driveway through evergreen trees and shrubs. Its outlook was very English too. Terraced lawns and rose gardens formed an apron between the building and the paddocks at its feet.

The house was built after the turn of the century, but the property had been in the hands of the Walter Shrimpton family for some time before that. It wasn't surprising really to find it reflecting so much English influence. Walter and his family came over from that sceptr'd isle as passengers aboard the *Charlotte Jane* and the *John Taylor*. They were two of the famous First Four Ships to hit the wharf at Lyttelton.

I'd like to have met that man, he sounded quite remarkable in many ways. He came from a highly respected printing and publishing family in England. But from what I could gather from all the confusing records of the day, most of them migrated with him to the Antipodes. Some went into the publishing business, setting up the Lyttelton Times for instance. Others went farming.

Incidentally, if anyone claims to have written a definitive history of the European settlement of New Zealand, don't believe a word of it. The records are a shambles.

So many of the brothers, uncles, cousins, and nephews of families that came in the early days, seemed to have the same first names. A favourite Christian name went the rounds of those big families like the Russian 'flu and the result was utter confusion.

Let's stick just to Walter, then. That's the Walter who built Matapiro. Not his uncle Walter or even his son Walter, who we'll come to later.

The Walter Shrimpton who stepped off the *John Taylor* at Lyttelton in 1853 was twelve years old. His father's name, thank goodness, was Ingram.

Now, apparently, Ingram wasn't too happy with the standard of schooling in the South Island at that time. So when Walt got to his teens, he had to face another ghastly sea voyage back to the UK. From then on, his life was one adventure after another.

It started with an academic stint which took him to Magdalen College, Oxford. Then he had a short maritime spell in the Royal Navy, followed by a longer one aboard a ship which took him back to New Zealand.

Back home, accompanied by his brother, he went exploring down south, looking for routes to the West Coast, naming the rivers Hope and Doubtless in the process. After that in turn he became a sheep farmer in Hawea, an officer in the militia on the Chathams and one of the first to bring wool off those islands commercially. He transported it by scow to the mainland. From all accounts, Walter must have been an enterprising lad.

When he was about thirty-three, he moved his interest to the North Island, marrying the daughter of one of three partners in the Matapiro estate. It was then a massive sheep station. His father-in-law's name was Rich, but he obviously didn't live up to it. Within a year, Walter had bought in and within another year he had bought the place outright.

From then on, it appears, he contented himself with a more settled life. Well there was plenty to do with almost 23,000 acres to look after. And the house hadn't been built yet, don't forget.

Maybe it never would have. Not the one I'd come to film on

its present location, anyway. But in 1898 his wife died and two years later, at the age of fifty-nine, Walter Shrimpton married again. This time, his bride was a young girl from New Plymouth.

With this marriage, he entered a new episode altogether. He became a father. In all, his wife bore him five children, but sadly, the son he gave his name to died at the age of six.

It must have been a blow indeed and the old man never ceased to express his feelings. When the new house was finished, part of the gardens was landscaped as a memorial. Set in the smooth, tailored lawns was a bed of roses of six varieties. The first letter of each variety spelt out the name of the boy.

He also donated funds for the establishment of a children's ward at Napier Hospital in memory of the child who'd been taken so prematurely. Ironically, the father, Walter senior, lived to the great age of ninety-six.

For years, the house had been unoccupied. By the family that is. As they grew up, they moved out and married. Or just moved out. Or died. Nevertheless, it had been kept in its original state. With all the original furnishings dusted and polished daily by a resident housekeeper and her husband.

When we were there, it was being administered by trustees. And so was the vastly reduced farm. But it wasn't entirely a museum of memories. Every so often it was brought back to life by visiting relatives.

The chief trustee, if there is such a thing, was Walter Shrimpton's daughter, Mrs Barbara Forde who farmed her own property a few miles down the road. She was our guide, a very charming and gracious one at that.

She was a busy lady, a widow in her late sixties, I suppose, but she always put herself at our disposal entirely. Indeed she was always there and ready to film before we were. She let me down in the end though. This genteel lady, who painted delicate landscapes, pulled a Hilda Alexander on me.

You see my plan was to make the closing shot of each house a zoom out. In that way, after seeing all the details and features individually, the viewer could see the house in its entirety and in its setting. In some cases, we could accomplish the filming from a high point on a nearby hill or building. But for others I wanted it done from a helicopter.

So, on the final day, we were all down in the paddock waiting for the helicopter to arrive. My cameraman had asked me if 1 would be going up first to take a look around and decide exactly what I wanted. What angle and so forth.

Well, I'd never flown in a helicopter before and although I was slowly getting over my natural fear of flying, I really wasn't too keen. I was just beginning to tell him how I didn't think it was necessary for me to go up. That, of course, I could trust him to get the shots I needed and so on, waffle, waffle, waffle, when the lady chipped in. "I'd certainly like to have a ride when he comes. Do make sure and get him to take me up, won't you." Once again I was sunk.

It didn't help one bit when the "chopper" arrived either. The pilot had obviously been in a dreadful accident at some time. His face was a patchwork of plastic surgery. This was the guy whose hands I was putting my life in. The one who was going to take me up. But of course, with this gentle old lady farmer standing watching with a challenging glint in her eye, I had no choice.

Everyone I've ever spoken to has always raved about the experience. There's nothing like it, they say. Well bully for them. I didn't get a heck of a lot more pleasure from levitating in that machine than I did from flying on the wing of the Tiger Moth.

Surrounded only by a thin sheet of glass, I felt like a bird suspended in space. Without wings. Expecting to drop like a lead weight at any time. The noise is something else too. It is quite impossible to communicate with anyone while you're up there. Especially not the grinning, scarred, air jockey who was first skimming tree tops by about a half a millimetre then elevating at a mile a second.

When I got down and Barbara Forde took my place, I learned that the pilot was "one of the best in the business, though he likes a bit of adventure". This information came from his mate who'd arrived with him from Napier. Apparently our fun-lover had survived a hell of a crash and been burned badly in the process. But his spirit was unharmed. I could vouch for that.

Thank goodness I hadn't arranged a helicopter shot for our next house. It's a very expensive way to film and of course, every shot counts. As things turned out it would have been nothing more than a flamboyant way of throwing our money away. You see, most of the film we shot at Akitio was ruined in processing by the dear old National Film Unit.

It was a shame really, we had such a pleasant time shooting it. We were made completely welcome and comfortable in the house by the owners, who insisted that we stay there for the filming. Everything went so well. Our hostess even washed our shirts. We really thought we were ahead this time. No accommodation or food expenses, no travelling, lots of time to work. What could be better. We hadn't considered the possibility of another "unexpected contingency".

We didn't learn of the fate of the film until a couple of weeks later. While we were on location, of course, we went sublimely along assuming that everything was just fine. Right on schedule, we turned up to film the massive Beetham residence, Brancepeth.

It really was massive too. When I asked the sheep-farmer owner how many rooms it had, the colourful Hugh Beetham replied: "I don't really know, Hanafi, there are quite a lot though."

He wasn't kidding either. I counted thirty that I could get doors open to. Mind you they weren't all in use. At least two of them seemed to be full of cardboard boxes and junk. Others were furnished as guest rooms, some with all the luxury of the past, including the porcelain wash bowl and jug and the giant pot.

In all, the house encompassed 10,000 square feet. On the ground floor a great deal of the space was taken up by the biggest hallway I'd ever seen. It was manorial.

Through two sets of heavy wooden doors, it suddenly opened up like an empty cathedral. Straight ahead, above panelled rimu, a row of stained glass windows depicting family mottoes were guarded each side by giant stags' heads. Up a bit too high to toss your cap onto though.

On one side, a wide staircase literally swept down from heaven above. Or more accurately from where the bedrooms and the cardboard boxes were on floor two. Actually the hallway and landing up there was bigger than most homes and their sections. The place was big in every sense of the word and all made from heart rimu milled right on the property. It even had a castellated tower. With a flag flying yet. The Beetham crest fluttered proudly I can tell you. Who says there's no money in sheep?

Really, Hugh Beetham should have been a thirteenth century English knight. Only the suit of armour and the horse were missing. Medium height, thick set, with his jaw jutting out, the fifty-six-year-old master of Brancepeth walked like a military commander looking for a battle.

So too had his ancestors apparently. Unfortunately, though, they were on the losing side at one of history's best known skirmishes. The battle of Bosworth Field. It seems that particular little *contretemps* didn't only decide the destiny of a king or two. It sealed the fate of the Beethams. They were deprived of their castle and lands.

However the New Zealand branch of the family did have a castellated tower, even if it was made of wood. By crikey, Hugh Beetham was proud of his heritage. I expected to have to stand for a toast at any time when we were talking together. Especially when we were deep in our leather chairs in his study. This was another gargantuan sized room. Wood-panelled and book-lined, it was Hugh's favourite room. He loved every inch of it. From the royal blue carpet with its gold *fleur de lis* pattern to its cigar smoke stained ceiling. His chair was right beside a huge open fireplace.

This was where, glass in hand, the owner of Brancepeth held court. With anyone. And anyone was welcome. The doors were always open. And if you dropped by and managed to pass the owner's coldly appraising stare you were in. The chances are that you'd then be whisked through to the kitchen for a feed, and then enticed into the study for a drink and a chat.

Hugh Beetham loved to chew the cud. So for that matter did his wife "Snooks" Beetham. She didn't play second fiddle for too long either. An attractive woman with dark curly hair, brown eyes and a dry sense of humour, she knew everyone. Well, everyone in the landowning business worth knowing anyway.

Whenever her husband slipped into the library for a snort and a chat, Snooks was never long in joining him. Before too long, the stories and anecdotes would be flowing and the laughs would come in bursts. Particularly from Hugh. His favourite expression, after he'd revealed some confidence or other to you was: "Don't talk to me about Basil Brush. What!" Whereupon, he'd roar with laughter. Sounding exactly like the voice of that furry character. But he could be very serious too. Especially when he talked about his ancestors. Then all the pride of the true aristocrat came out.

In the long, regal, dining room, we were admiring some of his forebears on the walls. "That's William Beetham, the artist who was a portrait painter. He was my great grandfather who was with the Royal Academy of Art. And that's a self-portrait by himself."

I seemed to have heard that expression somewhere before I felt. But I didn't follow it up. It wouldn't have paid to joke about that joker to Hugh.

Indeed it was great-grandfather Beetham, the portrait painter who was with the Royal Academy of Art, who brought the blood to New Zealand. It came in 1855, when he, his wife Mary and nine of their ten children arrived and settled in the Hutt Valley. They bought a piece of land there from the Maori Chief Wi Tako.

Anyway, before long, three of the sons had made their way over the Rimutakas and bought up some 90,000 acres of bush. That's how the sheep farming dynasty got started. After the clearing and a profitable little milling business of course. When we filmed, the property had shrunk to 3,500 acres. The original house had seen a few changes too. However, part of it, the study-cum-library was in a wing that dated back to 1886. After our filming at Brancepeth, the six house series really lost a lot of its interest and fun. For several reasons.

The news that we'd lost a whole programme through a processing blunder hurt us badly financially. Not only that though. It also meant that we had to find an extra house to film. At short notice.

As it was, my wife had covered many miles and interviewed dozens of mansion owners already and nothing looked too bright. Oh, sure, there were plenty of houses throughout Canterbury, some of them extremely big and fascinating, but as I mentioned earlier, most of them wouldn't play our game. Their owners weren't as public spirited as their northern counterparts.

Time and our budget were ebbing away rapidly as the search went on and the correspondence flew back and forth. "Sorry, we feel that the house has been given too much publicity already." That would be a reference to a back page spread in a Waimate weekly. "But we do look forward to the series," they usually ended sweetly. Or "Thank you for thinking of us for your programmes. Certainly our place is steeped in history and the forty-five rooms would be wonderful to see. However we're not at all happy about the outside appearance just now. So many of our wonderful pines that stood in the front have been knocked down in the recent storm. We reluctantly have to say no. For the present time anyway."

And so they came in. It got to the point that any positive answers, even if the house was built well into the twentieth century, were followed up personally.

In the end, instead of filming houses of my choice, I had to make do with ones close to home. In at least two of the three cases we settled for, the owners had very good reasons for welcoming us.

The first one, a medium-sized mansion with built-in servants' quarters, an outside pool, a complete wing for the billiards-room and a top-storey ghost, wanted the publicity.

The house was Wairewa, set on a sheep station in the picturesque countryside of Banks Peninsula. Its owner at that time was a youngish guy named Bill Latham, a grandson of the man who built it in 1902.

The house was quite nice in its way. A big brown and white wooden farmhouse in fact. But neither the furnishings nor the size of the rooms were exactly breath-taking. However, it was open for tourists. In fact busloads of them were transported up the long, winding driveway through the bush, to be taken for a cramped tour of the house. It didn't take long, because there weren't that many rooms. But the visitors loved it. Especially the scones and tea at the end.

Another place that wanted the publicity, we discovered, was a massive brick mansion called Racecourse Hill. After we'd arranged to film that one, we found out that the house was on the market and would soon be offered at auction.

We did a good job on it too and didn't even get offered a percentage. I tell you those South Island farmers are canny folk.

CHAPTER NINE

We Live Ourselves

"THE OLD WORLD IS DYING. Smothered in its own wealth and produce. Starving because of the exhausted resources. But a new generation, only a few, like the single or few sperms of an ejection, will survive and bear fruit. We are on the threshold of a new world, a fresh start, a new beginning. Some of the hippies, alternative people, freaks, rebels, will survive. We hope to be among them."

That statement was made to me in 1976, by Tim Vos, one of the most unusual people I ever met anywhere in New Zealand. I used the words, with their author speaking them, in the final scene of a documentary I made of his story. The filming took more than a year to complete and it was shown on television in late 1977.

I don't think the man ever claimed to be a prophet. The theme was an intrinsic part of his philosophy, rooted in religion. A conviction that had caused him to seek an alternative lifestyle many years earlier.

Since I first heard his thoughts, the world's industrialised nations have continued to stagger from one recession to another. Inflated prices have brought collapsing industries and unemployment. Fear has brought retrenchment and protectionism. Dwindling natural resources have buried international détente and caused east and west to focus on the Persian Gulf oil source like greedy dogs eyeing a piece of raw meat.

All over the globe, corruption and tyranny flourish; regulations and restrictions on human dignity and freedom have increased. Thousands of Asians suffering from malnourishment die daily. Humanity is often little more than dialectic. The age of materialism is complete. Why even the farmers of Invercargill got in a titch because they couldn't get their sheep into the local freezing works.

In the meantime, Tim Vos, the Dutchman who found his spiritual home on the West Coast of the South Island, has continued to do his thing; to survive and retain his independence.

I first met him in 1975, although I knew of him for some time before that. A friend of mine had worked as a postie with him in Christchuch in the 1960s. He told me to look out for the man if ever I went over to the Coast. So I did.

When I was researching for some other programmes over there, I made a point of seeking him out. To get to him, I had to make the long journey right up the coast road that winds, climbs and drops from Westport to Karamea. I was looking for a place called Corbyvale.

Actually, I hardly knew what to look for. The only instructions I had, were, "When you come down from the bluff and turn the bend, you'll see the old house on your right. That's Tim's place. It's the only house around, you can't miss it."

The person who gave me the directions didn't know my fallibility when I had to combine driving with navigation. I am probably the only man in New Zealand capable of missing Auckland after driving north from Hamilton. I cannot explain how I do it, but I do it.

On one famous occasion, I was actually living in Auckland and I'd driven down to Hamilton to play soccer. I was with my wife and family in a terrible car I'd not long bought and which had broken down, both going there and coming back.

Anyway, we got to some point about twenty miles or so from the centre of Auckland when I went wrong. It was dark by then and that probably helped to confuse me, although it really is no excuse. You see, instead of finding myself on the motorway, hurtling along those last few miles, I was driving further and further into deep dark countryside. In the end, when I realised that the turn-off to Greenlane wasn't going to come up, I stopped to ask for directions at a farm. Fortunately, the farmer had heard of Auckland and he managed to direct us back to the motorway.

What makes the whole thing even more absurd, is the fact that I'd driven to Hamilton and back many, many times before then. It is a straight road. When someone else is at the wheel that is.

In my later search for the residence of Tim Vos I was having to look out for a house in the middle of the bush and paddocks of the most remote part of the West Coast. Fortunately, though, the only turn-offs on that particular route will either lead you into the side of the hills, or into the Tasman Sea. Either way, you know you've gone wrong fairly soon.

It was drop-out country. Every so often, the rear end of an old truck or an old hippie, peeping from the bushes, told you so. There must have been dozens of young people over there at one time, seeking to escape the city pressures. Growing their hair and their marijuana to forget all their worries.

There were a couple of communes too, the bane of the local council and health authorities. One was just across the bridge over the Fox River. It was marked clearly to the traveller by a huge geodesic dome up on the hillside. That building didn't cause any concern though. Nobody lived in it. It was a workshop and studio for a potter and others in the group. No it was an old railway carriage home that didn't pass the local regulations. Well, not for domestic living quarters anyway.

I managed to find the Vos homestead without too much trouble. I only overshot it by a few yards at first. Sure enough, it was the only house around when you twisted down from View Hill saddle, some 1400 feet above the sea.

The setting was magnificent. A row of pines shielded the property from the westerly winds and the strangers' gaze. The eye is deflected away. On the opposite side of the road, incredibly green pasture-land breaks free from the shadows of the hills. And cutting away at right angles to the road, a bubbling creek divides the two terrains.

The natural beauty wasn't just one-sided though. The Vos house sat amidst a similar scene behind the pines. The black corrugated iron sheathed building was bounded on one side by thick bush clad hills and on the other by the creek. Beyond the creek were more paddocks and, where the icy water sprang, more trees and hills.

In fact the land was a gradual slope from the moment you left the road, crossed over the little wooden bridge and walked up the stony path to the house.

The only way to enter in the front, would have been through the window. It had a door, but like the windows it was suspended above the ground. There was a large gap between it and a set of stone steps. Obviously a verandah at one time had closed that gap, but in its absence, the door was no longer used. A path led round the side to the back. That's where I first met the family Vos. All of a bustle.

It was a bit like a courtyard round there, with outbuildings dripping with old farm implements. Tools, milk buckets, saws, axes, harnesses, ancient scythes, plough parts and swingletrees. Everything in fact that the modern farmer of the 1850s would need to break in the land and run a farm efficiently.

In, on top of, and around it all, chickens pecked, doves perched or fluttered and cats lay curled. Then children appeared. From the creek, from inside the house, from the hills beyond another row of pines. Blond, round faced, curious. Big red setter dogs bounded across the scene barking and leaping and then, from the murky darkness of one of the outbuildings the black-bearded master appeared. He had a hammer in his hand. He was busy and he lost no time at all in telling me so either.

I'd come at the worst possible time. The family was preparing to leave its home temporarily. Tim was working like mad to get things ready for the trip. When I introduced myself and explained that I was a television producer, he was even more abrupt. He'd had too many interruptions from people dropping by and he really had to get on with his work. He intended taking his family and his animals to drier pasture for the winter. He was preparing for a mini exodus.

Corbyvale has the heaviest rainfall in the country. In some months the place is a quagmire. It becomes so sodden the potatoes rot in the earth. So, the family was off to a more protected spot, where it would camp under canvas until the seasons changed.

For the journey, the man would travel by bullock-drawn cart with his horse, his sheep, his goats and his dogs running behind. In the cart would be his wife and six children, their chickens, doves, cats, their tent and all the cooking utensils they could pile in. Not forgetting a sack of wheat, some mollasses and their guns.

My presence was not only incongruous, it was not welcome. Right then I was interrupting his work on fashioning new shafts for the small cart he had. The whole scene was too fascinating to walk away from though. If I'd had a camera with me, I would have been shooting from the moment I walked in. As it was, I could see I had to be very careful. This man had turned away from the very lifestyle that I represented, in its crassest form. He sought an alternative to the normal social environment of the city. I brought it all back with me in my collar and tie.

Tim Vos was standing with his hand on the latch of the back door to his home. Waiting to go in. But first he was waiting for me to go away. I had to play my ace. I told him I brought greetings from his old postie colleague in Christchurch. It was true. Both the man and his wife had asked me to convey their best wishes if I should ever meet up with Tim Vos. It did the trick.

Within minutes, I was on the inside of the house, sitting near a massive open fireplace, talking to the man from Corbyvale. And his wife Jos. And the children, from the eldest, fourteen-year-old Daniel, to the youngest, six-year old Kester. And the dogs. And a couple of cats. And the doves. And a few hens. In fact I wouldn't have been in the least bit surprised to see the odd sheep stroll through. They were a very close family. When that back door got opened, it was either all out or all in, together.

Once I was inside the house, I was treated as a guest, with warmth and hospitality. Tim really liked company, and amidst his family, he soon revealed more than a hint of his zealous attitude towards everything he did.

He was about thirty-nine-years old, I suppose, though he had the lithe wiry frame of a man twenty years younger. There wasn't a spare ounce of fat anywhere. He also had the impatient exuberance of youth. Hard to keep still. A handsome man, with fine features, the Dutchman had shining blue eyes, a mass of dark wavy hair and an old testament beard. His costume that day, was one I was to see many times later. A dark blue roll-neck sweater, rough leather shorts and a pair of old gumboots.

His wife, Jos, was about five years younger than Tim and she had the gentle but strong mien of the countrywoman. She wore her long flaxen hair pulled back and tied behind her head. She was a biggish girl, much heavier than before her child-bearing days, I guessed, but she had a youthful, joyful spirit and a terrific feeling of peace. And she was handsome too. Certainly her bright green eyes and fair skin needed no makeup to assist them.

They were quite a pair in fact. Jos wore the long dress of the pioneer wife with a Dutch smock over the top. But the room we sat in echoed the past even more than the people did.

It had the austere simplicity of the pioneering days, along with an aesthetic style that was unmistakeably European. I felt as if I were sitting in the middle of an old Dutch painting. In the centre, a massive fire stack dominated the room. It was the centre, separating the kitchen area from the rest like a huge wide pillar. Each side had a yard or so of space to walk by or around it.

We sat on hard wooden chairs with our backs to a big oak table, warming our feet and airing our knowledge. On one side of the room doors led to other parts I would learn about later. On the other side, the thinning afternoon light found its way through dainty lace curtains. Soon the kerosene lamps would have to be lit. Above us, the high ceiling dripped with more old farm tools and implements, gathering dust and soot from the fire below.

Our first meeting was a little tentative initially. We were all feeling each other out, looking for common ground. Something we could all communicate freely about. Inevitably, it was religion and the family. We discussed our beliefs in both, but a little warily. I felt as if I would have to prove my sincerity in order to win the man's trust. When I mentioned the possibility of doing a film, the idea met with mixed feelings. Right then wasn't the best time to go into details. I asked if l could come back and bring someone with me.

A few weeks later, I was filming on the Coast, so I decided to see if the family were still at home. I wanted my cameraman and unit manager to see what I'd seen, to verify my excitement about a possible film.

They had not yet left. Victims of too many visitors, I discovered. Indeed when we turned up, there were several other people in the house. Friends from the Fox River commune I was told as I was introduced to them all. The conversation was not as free as I'd hoped. There seemed to be a blockage. The opters-out from the commune heightened the difference between the family and their lifestyle and my crew, myself and what we represented.

Tim was considered something of a leader on the Coast. His resolution and determination were admired and his almost evangelical denunciation of the "rat race" and the corrupting influences of modern society warmed his audiences. And he loved an audience. He'd be the first to admit it at that time. He virtually preached the alternative way, along with the warnings of the Bible. After a while, we saw something of this side of Tim Vos. He spoke with the flow of a man inspired. A religious zealot. His eyes sparkled as he talked of throwing off the shackles of so-called progress and science and returning to the land. To his Maker.

In that atmosphere, in that company, it was difficult for him to appear to agree to any filming. But, slowly, gradually, he and I were coming closer. When I left, I had the family's assurance that I was the only person on earth that they would allow themselves to be filmed by. Even so, it would have to wait. I wasn't ready then and they were all set to migrate for a few months.

It must have been a year later that the subject was broached again. By mail. Many things had happened in the meantime. For both of us. Jos's mother who had come from Holland to join them, had died. But as so often happens as one life leaves, another was on the way. Jos was with child for the seventh time. For my part, I'd left the safety of the corporation completely, so, in Tim's eyes, I was a good deal more respectable. We would meet to discuss the film.

This time, I travelled from Christchurch to the Coast with the three other directors of Telenion Productions. We would all see for ourselves something of the project in view. On this trip, we booked in at a motel in Karamea so that we could spend plenty of time talking, getting used to each other and looking at all likely locations.

The first night, Tim told us his story. Well some of it.

His desire to be different, to live his own way, had been spawned in childhood in Holland. He'd attended a free method school, where, incidentally, he'd met Jos. In their teens they had been sweethearts. Later, while Jos studied art to become an accomplished tapestry weaver, Tim had gone to sea. He was first mate in the Dutch merchant service, travelling all over the world. When he left the service he married his childhood girlfriend and they set up home on a houseboat, selling craft goods. But then he started to find life in Holland stifling. In 1964, he, his wife and their two children, Daniel and Joella emigrated to New Zealand.

They settled in Christchurch, attempting at first to live the conventional life they saw around them. In fact, Tim said he really fancied becoming bourgeois. They were tempted to buy such wonders of technology as a refrigerator, an electric sewing machine, even a tape recorder and record player. At this time, Tim was on the assembly line in a Christchurch factory. But it didn't work. Instead of enjoying the world of material comforts, they found it heavy and unfulfilling.

The next stage found them trying a compromise. Tim got a job as a postie and their domestic lifestyle took on some changes. More children were coming along, so he started to acquire some animals to feed them. Sheep and goats were added to his menagerie of domestic pets and chickens. Not just a couple of each either. A dozen of each was more like it. And they needed space to graze.

It soon became obvious that this mini farm couldn't be contained in his back section. It was, after all, just a regular garden attached to just a regular three-bedroomed house. So Tim took to the hills. Literally. He led his flock of grass and shoot eaters onto the hills around the bay of Sumner or to any spare land he could find.

Now Sumner is a fairly sedate little suburb of Christchurch. What is usually described by real estate people as a "desirable area". It is right on the coastal beach, crowded, almost, by the hills that fringe it. Any spare land available, including the slopes, would be very adjacent to someone's property. Their little quarter acre sections. So naturally enough, there were complaints. Oh, there was a good deal of sympathy for the man who was striving to feed his rapidly expanding family, but when heads and teeth got through the fences, the neighbours were less altruistic.

Just the same, the family was experimenting with the kind of lifestyle they were later to adopt wholeheartedly. Tim was cutting scrub from the hills for firewood and Jos was burning it in the back garden to heat her copper and bake her bread. I'm not too sure what their neighbours thought of that either.

Altogether, the Voses lived in Christchurch for seven years and during that time they added four children to the family. However, as time went on, their unhappiness grew. They were uncomfortable with their environment. But if they were prepared to compromise where they lived, they were unable to compromise their principles. So they often ran into pain.

For instance, the eldest boy, Daniel, was suffering quite a bit in the process of carrying out Christian beliefs instilled in him by his father. The local schoolmaster warned Tim that it didn't pay to turn the other cheek when someone thumped you. Not in today's playground scene. But the father insisted and the conflict in his soul grew bigger and bigger. He felt he was losing control of his family; that society's pressures were taking over and insisting on standards different from those he believed in. However, he was a man of faith. Of considerable faith. So he turned to the one place he hoped would answer his cry. He prayed for enlightenment.

It all sounds a little dramatic, I suppose, in conventional terms. Most people use the concept of God to acquire something. Tim was praying to be divested of something. He desperately wanted a change.

His answer came in the form of a dream. A very vivid dream in which he was driving a car down a road he'd never seen before, chasing a big yellow vehicle. In it, he felt, was something that had been taken away from him. Something that was very dear to him that he was striving to retrieve. In the dream, he seemed to drive through a cloud of dust across the road. When he had gone through it, he saw a grey car coming towards him. As they passed, the man at the wheel waved to him. He didn't recognise the face.

The effect of the dream had been profound. Tim felt the man symbolised something that would take him out of the frustration of trying to hold on to what was his. He was convinced that his children should be influenced only by the family and that he had to provide the right environment for them. To do this he had to cut away from society and retain his own freedom. In that way, he reasoned, they would know what freedom was for themselves. But, how?

He started to look around the country for a place to escape to. His search took him to Marlborough and the romantic Sounds. He was apparently very attracted to the area but found nothing he could afford. Then unexpectedly, he heard from his brother, Tom. He'd rented a small farm near

Karamea for the family. If they wanted it, they should come right away.

Tim's brother was a loner. A bachelor, who tended to roam all over the place with a similar disregard for life's comforts as Tim. He'd known of the family's frustrations and was certain that the place for them was on the West Coast. Now it was up to them. At first, the idea didn't appeal too much, I gather. However the alternative of staying in Sumner was far worse. So they sold the house and headed west.

I'd like to have been there on moving day. It must have been an interesting sight. What with all the animals lining up to get into a truck along with the furniture and tools. You see, Tim had used the equity from the sale of his house and a vintage car he'd owned to indulge his great love. He'd bought as many old farm implements and tools and old cooking utensils as he could find. The furniture was magnificent too. It included a genuine leather four piece suite and a full size loom. Whether or not the animals were allowed to sit or perch on the furniture during the journey, I couldn't tell you. But the kids weren't. They travelled down in a rented car.

Sumner must have missed that eccentric family, as they set off for the adventure of their lives. Turning the clock back and living off the land completely.

Unfortunately, initially at least, the notion proved to be a bit too romantic, even for the West Coast. The farm they moved into was small and provided little more than grazing for their animals and a roof over their heads. Also it had a rent that had to be paid. So straightaway, Tim had to get work to support it. He started in the local sawmills. But once again, it all seemed wrong. He was, he said, back in the same old rat race.

The climax came when it was time for the children to attend school. The move from the city had been made during the summer holiday and now it was over. On the first morning, the three children old enough to go ran out and caught the school bus. They were in a rush. Too much of a rush, because they'd left their lunches behind. Jos ran out after them but she was too late, so she asked Tim to try to catch up with them.

Fortunately, he still had the car he'd rented to bring them to the Coast, so he jumped in and gave chase. Then his dream took over in reality. As he got near the bus, the yellow bus, he was faced with a cloud of dust from its wheels. When he got through the dust, a grey car was coming towards him. At the wheel was the face in his dream. The man waved. Tim could hardly believe what was happening.

Anyway, he caught up the bus and delivered the lunch packs and then returned to the farm, wondering about his experience. Outside his house was the grey car. The one he'd passed on the road.

Inside was the man who owned it. The man who'd waved as they passed. He was real then. Indeed, he was another Dutchman. His name was Peter de Vries and he was one of the rangers responsible for the Heaphy Track: the rugged tramp that runs from just north of Karamea across to Bainham in Golden Bay on the island's north-east coast. He'd called to say hello. No more. But he was to supply the key to the rest of Tim's story. He was to prove the vital link that would take the family to the freedom they sought. The man was quizzed about any possible available land in the district that might be leased cheaply. There was nothing... except maybe, he couldn't be sure, but there just could be the possibility of some in an isolated place down the coast. From a helicopter at one time he'd seen a spread of green. Between the Kongahu reserve lands and the sea. The only way to it though was over craggy boulders and outcroppings when the vicious tide was out.

Tim needed little prompting. He made the journey to inspect it and fell in love with the country. A local farmer had some stock down there and de Vries had suggested that Tim approach him. So he did.

Could he lease the land? No. Could he buy it? No. Could he squat on it? O.K. That was enough.

Everything seemed to be working out. The man in the car had shown him how to break free from his frustration. Where to find his freedom. Tim is a man of great enthusiasm. In retelling his story, five years later, he lost none of the excitement that he felt at the time. It was God's guidance to the family.

But it was in a hell of a spot. Tim soon realised that. He'd tried the jaunt along the sea coast. Fine for a strong tenacious man when the tide was out, but not for a family. Not for the sheep and the goats and the dogs and the cats and the chickens and the doves. Nor the loom and the leather suite of furniture. No way. It was tantalising. The land was good. Fresh and green. But it was virtually inaccessible to him. Unless he could penetrate the daunting bushland. It was his only hope.

In preparation for his second migration, he brought all his belongings to an old hut on the beach at Little Wanganui. The one-time port was at the northern end of the vast area of scenic reserve and crown land that "hogged" the coast for miles.

From his new camp, Tim started to survey the terrain. Studying the run of the river, looking for signs of old tracks. For more than two months he tried to find a way into and through what must be some of New Zealand's most rugged country. The one track he'd found proved to be hopeless. It went from sea level to 1300 feet and then down to sea level again.

It was a time of trial for the family. They had very little to eat and they were living on the child allowances only. They had to suffer criticism from the locals and even people they'd known back in Christchurch. The child welfare department sent messengers out and friends sent food parcels. But Tim couldn't give up. He might have, he said, but for the dream. It sustained him through all the torment and shortage.

Finally, his luck broke. He came upon an old cadastral map of the district. It showed clearly that there had been a road right through the Kongahu. Not only that. It must have been a good road. There had been a community linked by it and carts must have used it to bring out timber and dairy produce for the markets.

The problem was, though, that the area had felt the impact of the 1929 Murchison earthquake. It had changed the face of the place. What the earth movement on that occasion hadn't done to demolish traces of the road, subsequent storms, bringing slips and torn down trees, had. In the meantime too, new growth had sprung up all around and engulfed its shattered remains.

But the road had existed and it had a start and an end. It must have stretched for about eight miles.

Until he found the map, Tim had been searching the hills and valleys where the road must have emerged. So next he went to where it must have started. To the tableland known as Corbyvale. Just off the main, tar-sealed coast road was the original source. Its course ran alongside a wire fence separating two paddocks for half a mile before it entered the heavy dark bush.

He had found it! And he followed as far as he could, marvelling more and more as he discovered its route. It wasn't easy going. Logs like houses lay tangled across its path and landslips had all but erased it. But the signs persisted. Mosses on the banks and half-buried wood corduroying guided him on until he realised that there was a way through.

However, he also had to accept that as a track, it was navigable only by an inspired explorer. Sure there had been a road. Certainly it was possible to retrace its course. But before it could possibly be considered as a way of getting from A to B, it would need to be rebuilt. Bridges would have to be made across creeks. Trees would have to be felled. Rock and tree trunks would have to be blasted aside with dynamite and new footings established in the hillsides.

Nothing, though, could diminish Tim's excitement at that time. Nothing could detract from his sense of discovery. As he put it:

"I saw the great gift of it. Then my mind went berserk. I was raving about it. I said, 'My! Here is the highway!' And it was struggling under mud and under all this undergrowth and it took almost two days to come back and forth along that road. In many places you got lost. You got in the bush and never find your way back and you have to stay out there. That bad it was. But still, I had this blowing my mind. I was saying, that's going to be the Vos Avenue."

Tim had discovered what was still, officially, a public road. The Spenser Road. The long forgotten artery through the Kongahu. But that's not all. He planned to make it a live artery again and he had stumbled on something that could help his dream come true.

Immediately across from the paddocks where the road began, he'd spotted the abandoned shell of a house. It had been the homestead for one of the fistful of farms that once peppered the area. When the Dutchman saw it the building was derelict, with cows wandering in and out.

To Tim, it was a Godsend, perfectly situated for all his needs. Around it, the bush bulged with fuel for his fires. Alongside it a rapidly running creek would provide his water needs. There was even grazing space for his animals. But perhaps even more important it would provide him with an excellent base for his monumental task in reclaiming the Spenser Road.

The owner of the property lived in Westport, so a compassionate local mail-van driver spoke to him on Tim's behalf. Could the family squat in his old shack whilst they rebuilt the road? The idea was insane, but the alternative was too much for the farmer to countenance. The driver told him that the mad Dutchman was so determined in his aim that if he couldn't use the house he would take his family into the bush and live there.

The owner said he was thinking of putting a match to the building because it was little more than an eyesore. But, if the Dutchman wanted it then he could go ahead and squat there. Perhaps in exchange he could keep an eye on the farmer's stock in the process.

Tim had his home and his freedom.

That had all happened five years before we sat in his lounge talking about making a film. By then, three miles of the road had been opened up and could be walked on safely.

The house that had been on the brink of demolition had seen some changes too. Tim had ripped out walls, rebuilt, extended, strengthened. The roof had been torn off in a gale and replaced in a frenzy by the inspired tenant. The hulk had been reinforced and weather-proofed by corrugated-iron covered with tar. The outbuildings had been added to with a "dunny" room and a home-made A-frame. This last building I came to know intimately, later. With very mixed feelings.

I can't imagine how anybody could have chosen a tougher battlefield to fight for his freedom. When we talked in 1976 much of the battle was over, but the previous years' experiences must have tested Tim Vos to the very limit. That part could never be filmed as a documentary. In a way, I felt cheated. If ever there'd been a story of determination to overcome incredible difficulties, the Vos family had lived it. In seeking an alternative way, they had chosen to turn the clock back and endure all the hardship, backbreaking labour and doubts of a pioneer family.

When the family and all their various animals moved into Corbyvale they brought with them two sacks of wheat, a drum of molasses and some tins of honey. That was their storehouse. That's what they had to live on. The wheat was ground for porridge and mixed with molasses for bread. When they discovered watercress growing in the creek and a few herbs in the paddock, they rejoiced. They had some vegetables. Sometimes, they even had meat. Maybe a sheep would be sacrificed. But mostly it would be possum in the pot.

Many times though, they really had to improvise. When the wheat ran out, they tried the pith of the punga and king ferns for instance. "We didn't get hungry," said Tim, "but we came to the stage where we ate the same food as the goats ate.

There is a time here in Corbyvale that even the creeks run out of watercress. Then we just grind in the meat mincer whatever young shoots the goats are eating. And so I say, we never got hungry because it's the best food there is. It's very healthy food. But, well, we had to chew on it..."

What to put in their stomachs wasn't the only problem they faced either. They weren't exactly welcomed into the valley by the local conventional farmers of the district. They were the unknown, the gypsies, and therefore something to be wary of and distrusted. One man in particular gave Tim a hard time.

As soon as work got underway on clearing the 'road', the Dutchman applied to the Lands Department for some of the land alongside it. Something he could build on and farm perhaps. Apparently, parts of the old pre-earthquake properties were still in fair shape and there was evidence of rich grazing land. Tim was providing access to it.

The government department wasn't impressed though. Not for a long time anyway. But as I've said before, the man was a very determined character, so he persisted. Eventually, they gave in and granted him the land he'd seen. But only for grazing. Under the terms of the lease offered to him, he would not be allowed to erect any kind of permanent building. Also the lease could be terminated at the drop of a new government plan for the area.

It wasn't quite what Tim was hoping for, but it was good news anyway. At least he would have somewhere to graze his animals. By that time, they'd pretty well picked his little plot of grass down to below the roots. But it wasn't to be. As soon as he took his long haired sheep and short haired goats onto the place, he discovered his neighbour could talk. Could even shout.

The man claimed that the land was his by right of usage. He said he sometimes "spelled" his own paddocks by driving his cattle through the bush onto it. Tim was told to get his animals off. When the Dutchman refused and pointed out that he had a legal right to the place, the farmer went berserk. He tried to physically assault Tim and threatened to shoot him. It had been a harrowing experience for a man who hated violence.

He told me how the big farmer, black with anger, had grabbed him by the front of his shirt so fiercely that Tim had slipped out of the garment and fallen to the ground.

It sounded funny when he told the story, but the effect of the threats and intimidation were profound at the time. So much so that the squatter who'd been legally given his own land, had to turn it down. He returned to the Lands and Survey Department and pleaded with them to take it back and give him something else. He told them he didn't want to be shot over a piece of earth.

Reluctantly, the government office took back the rights. There was little else they could offer in return. Just some sour, swampish bush about a mile and a half from his house and a fine piece of inaccessible land on the crest of a mighty hill some six miles away. Near the end of the old Spenser Road. Each piece was about a hundred acres. Tim settled for both. At least no one would want to fight him for either. The nearest piece, he hoped to clear and open up to the sun. It would be the source of future fuel for his hungry fire. When it was cleared, it would provide grazing for his flock. The second plot was intended for grander plans. That is where, one day, he would settle and build.

Never mind the restriction of the lease, the man decided, he would build a place that anyone could share. A palatial tramper's hut. That would get over the by-laws. But first he had to get there. Again the challenge of rebuilding the old public road. Now he had even greater incentive than before.

In any other part of New Zealand, with chainsaws and bulldozers, it would have presented quite a task. On the West Coast, with one man and his son working only with hand tools, it looked like a lifetime's labour. Whatever progress was achieved was often washed away by the torrential rains that constantly deluged the area.

But Tim refused to give up hope. He'd live in that massive

bush area one day, he swore. And he expected many others to join him there. In fact he dreamed of a new community living along the length of the reclaimed road. A society of likeminded people who would live off the land and turn their backs on "scientific progress".

In the meantime, every day of their lives was an adventure for the Vos family. The only security they had was their faith, their dreams and two patches of bush owned by the Crown. At anytime they could be asked to leave their refuge by the creek in Corbyvale.

They had known despair and joy. And when we sat and talked of the past, their enthusiasm was as keen as it had ever been. I almost had to restrain Tim from telling me of all the things he planned to do which we could film. A documentary film could encompass only so much.

It was almost enough for me to be able to capture something of their daily lifestyle. To show the way the individual members of the family interrelated. To see the goats being milked. And the new arrival, a milking cow. To watch Jos boiling up her clothes in her copper by the creek. To see the watercress being gathered and the bread being baked. The correspondence school work, the possums being trapped, the trees being felled, the swamp being cleared and to show progress of the road building.

That in itself would make a fascinating film, I knew. It would be too much to ask to see the road finished and the family and animals being led to the new land on the hill. But that's what Tim tempted me with.

I planned to return at three monthly intervals over the course of a year. That way, we could record the progress and see the family grow up amidst the changes. It was agreed. Jos even suggested I could film the birth of the new baby. But it wasn't to be. Unfortunately, before I could get back to the coast to start work on the film, the baby had been born. However, Tim had more treats up his sleeve. He intended now to build a windmill.

Filming the story of the Vos family, I knew was going to be

the most difficult project I had ever attempted. Of course I couldn't just shoot a parade of passing images representing an unusual family's behaviour. I was endeavouring to capture a spirit, an essence, that I had seen manifesting itself in them. A quality that so many of the rest of us have either forgotten about or subjugated.

I think Jos summed up what I mean when I once asked her about the life in Corbyvale for her.

I had seen her with a wooden yoke around her neck, carrying two heavy buckets of water from the creek to the house. I had seen her sitting on rocks in the freezing water scrubbing away at muddy jeans. I'd watched her baking bread, weaving wool, milking the cow. I suggested to her that it was a strenuous life. I said one would have to be tough to live it. But Jos answered like this:

"No," she said, "I think it's more of making up your mind. It's not tough, because you've got no tensions what other people got in town. You can do everything what you want to do in a relaxed way. And it was just only making the decision if you want it or not. And we made that decision already in town. Because we felt it was too much we were not living ourself, but other people, they lived us. And that's so."

When she said it, I knew what the title of the film had to be. I called it "We live ourselves". And that's what I tried to convey. A group of people who lived themselves, guided by their own feelings. Their own individuality, released from the pressure of having to conform.

My biggest problem would be not to interrupt the natural flow of behaviour; to attempt to film things as they happened, as spontaneously as possible. When Tim talked of living on bread and watercress, that's what I wanted. I was hoping to achieve the impossible though. The only way to catch what I was after successfully would have been for me to become invisible and have an invisible camera set up all the time.

In the event, much of what I did must have puzzled and disturbed the family, however true we tried to be. I remember, for instance seeing one of the children fetching water from the creek. He was a wee chap of eight or so and the bucket was heavy. It spilled from time to time as he made his way to the house, totally concentrated on what he was doing. By the time the camera was ready to "snatch" the moment, the journey was completed and the water delivered. I asked the boy to repeat it. But he couldn't understand why. There was no need for more water. The motivation for the action would be unreal.

In some other instances, when I wanted something filmed that I knew to be a true activity, my insistence caused great pain. I had the dilemma always that I didn't want to labour anything, clog it with intellectual reasoning. However, to the mind of free-living creatures, my attitude could easily be interpreted as autocratic and domineering.

Over the long period that we filmed, we all got to know each other more and more of course. But in the process, I was cautious, lest my feelings got too involved. I had to witness, to interpret and like the man I was filming, I had to do it my way. Sometimes we clashed. Most of the time, the family gave everything of themselves and in return, they wanted the same from me.

It was a very unreal experience after all. This group of characters with their sophisticated equipment and city ideas would suddenly descend and take over their lives. Each day, they would wander around or organise things so that a camera could shoot what they wanted. Whenever a cloud came over in the middle of a shot, they had to do it again. What had happened to the Vos family's freedom?

They were incredibly patient, particularly since we were never totally with them. Although we tried that on one visit, to help overcome the brittle start and finish of every filming day. You see, on each trip, we booked into the motel in Karamea for a week or so. That meant that the delicate relationship between the filmers and the filmed had to be re-established every day.

At times this routine caused some strain. Particularly since I often have a habit of following my feelings too, instead of too much rigid pre-planning. Communication was often difficult whilst we camped so far away. So on one occasion we took up the family's offer to stay on the property, in the home-made A-frame.

Normally, the two Vos daughters slept in the building. So they moved out and back into the house, to make room. I wished they had refused to.

I think you really have to love the little place to live in it. That must have been my problem. It didn't really appeal to me from the start. Oh, it was structurally quite safe, despite the gaps here and there in the stone walls, but it was a trifle cramped and primitive. For my tastes anyway.

Tim had made it with boulders from· the creek, held together, sometimes, by cement. The actual floor area was about ten feet by five and a lot of that was taken up by inanimate objects.

A wood stove took care of one corner. An old treadle sewing machine had another. A chest of drawers occupied a third corner and along the wall from just inside the door, a wooden couch ran into the fourth.

In the middle of the room, there was a small table for us to eat at and running up from whatever space that was left, was a ladder to a loft. A triangular loft of course, because the two sides of the corrugated roof met up there. That's where I slept. The other three guys curled around in their sleeping bags down below. None too luxuriously. One on the bench and the other two on the floor.

Actually, I must admit, that I am a creature of comfort. I do tend to enjoy stretching out in a bed with an electric blanket on it or at least five hot water bottles. So although it wasn't exactly the Hilton penthouse, I wasn't unhappy when it was agreed that I get the top bunk. I think my age played in my favour to some extent. Plus the fact that when the sleeping arrangements were being discussed, I suddenly developed shooting pains throughout my back. The crew knew I had a history of sciatic agony. They should have done, I told them often enough.

However, on the second night of our stay in that rude hut, I regretted the deference I'd been shown very much.

It was a wet, cold night and we were all tired when we turned in. We'd had the old wooden stove going to cook up some tea and warm up the place. And we'd played a hand or two of cards in the dim kerosene light. It had been a good day's filming and everybody seemed happy that we were staying on the property each night. Even I did, until that night.

I was lying up in my loft, cocooned in my sleeping bag, Sleep had come easily, despite the hard boards. Partly because of fatigue. Partly because of the asphyxiating smoke from the stove below me. Anyway I was dozing heavily, when suddenly I felt something on my neck. I woke instantly, grabbing at the back of my head and throwing some object away from me. But what was it and where had it gone?

I groped around for a torch. In the dark, I had no idea which way I was facing. The thing I'd had on my neck felt substantial. I could either have thrown it against the wall, or through the gap opposite. In which case it could have landed on one of my colleagues below.

I shone the torch against the wall and all around. There was nothing there. Near the top was a square ventilation hole. Maybe it had flown or hoisted itself out through that aperture I thought. I was looking for something at least as big as a bat.

Next, I started to explore the rafters above my head, slowly, thoroughly, when, suddenly, I saw it. "Oh, my God!" I exclaimed. I'd never seen anything like it before in my life. But there it was all right. The creature looking down at me truculently was about four inches long. Its body appeared to be a mixture of blue and brown. Its head was round with a phosphorescent glow and its great eyes were watching my every move.

The beast was uncanny. It had great saw-toothed legs and hideous feelers at the top of its head like radio aerials. I had no choice. I yelled Ughh! Ughh! and rapidly made my way down the ladder to my friends below.

Suddenly the place was in tumult. I'd woken the lot with the last Ughh! as I had hoped. Now I was shuddering dramatically as I picked my way over their startled figures.

"What the hell's going on?" yelled one of them. I explained as coherently as I could. Then they were all up, curious to discover what this strange object was.

The soundman was the first to tackle the ladder. A no nonsense lad, Hammond Peek was a true grit Kiwi. As brave and adventurous as they come. He took a big torch with him though I noticed he went no further up than the third step from the top.

"There you are, you little bastard," he was speaking to the thing. "It's a weta, haven't you seen one of them before, Hanafi?" He was talking in the same tones that parents use for backward eight-year-olds.

"Not from Mars, no!" I retorted sharply. I was in no mood to discuss comparative entomological knowledge at that time of night. Certainly I'd seen wetas before. But nothing to even vaguely compare with that grotesque arthropod squatting above my now vacant sleeping bag.

"Where is it? Let's have a look at the swine?" Hamdani the cameraman was now on the ladder as Hammond came down.

"Give us the torch, where is it?" Mr Milas was searching the rafters. "Jesus!" he exclaimed. It was becoming a very religious experience.

Now Hammond was back on the ladder, this time armed with an axe. It would have been hilarious if the monster above hadn't been such a shock.

As soon as he was in striking distance, Hammond lashed out, egged on now by a fervent cameraman. "Kill the bastard. Go on Hammond. Smash the bastard!" he screamed as the steady thud, thud of the axe against wood shook the little A-frame.

Finally, Hammond descended victorious. He held the crippled creature limply by a leg, then opened the door and threw it outside. We all relaxed.

Meanwhile Ramzi, the unit manager, who was the one to claim the wooden couch for a bed, had laid low, I noticed. Alert, watchful, encouraging even but from a very low profile. Now he was up on his feet. "How about a cup of tea, then lads?" He had the excuse he needed.

We had our tea, joked about my cowardice and returned to our sleeping bags.

Next morning, the Vos family were curious indeed. They'd heard all the rumpus and wondered what on earth had happened. Apparently they weren't too keen on the local variety of wetas either. Anyway, by the end of another hard day of filming in the bush, we'd forgotten all about it. Until after tea.

I think I was washing up at the time. A careful balancing act in those cramped quarters it was too. Hammond was struggling in the pallid light, cleaning and fussing with his sound equipment. Hamdani was loading film into a camera magazine and Ramzi was in bed, on the couch. He'd complained of not feeling too well and decided to lie down in his sleeping bag. He was trying to read by the light of the oil lamp. Everything was quiet, until he moved. The unit manager, that is.

Suddenly, with nothing more than a gasp, Ramzi had moved from lying down on the couch to standing up in the furthest corner from it. Still in his sleeping bag.

"Take a look at that bloody thing. There, just above where my head was," he cried. We did.

Sure enough, there was another of those aliens. Just sitting vibrating on a cross bar of the wall, looking at us.

"Jesus, it's even bigger than the last one!" someone said.

"Hammond!" I uttered. He knew exactly what I meant. Again the axe went into action. Again my man from Picton demonstrated his complete fearlessness. Four powerful strokes from the axe and he had the four inch creature on its knees. The *coup de grace* followed swiftly and out the door it went, straight into the jaws of one of the dogs.

"Maybe we should have a little look around, boys," I

suggested. "If there are any more of those little fellows around I think I'll sleep in the back of the car."

"So will I." Ramzi was right there with me.

The inspection proved to be a very prudent move. We discovered an enormous spider, just above where the cameraman would be sleeping, and another weta. It was of the same genetic strain as the two extra-terrestrials we had disposed of. Worst still, it was upstairs where my bed was. "But not tonight, friends," I said, as I took my sleeping bag down, grabbed a torch and left for the car with the unit manager. It would be extremely uncomfortable in the back of the station wagon, but at least I wouldn't be harassed by monsters.

Fortunately, or unfortunately, I had to spend only two nights in the car. We had to cut our trip short and go home because of bad weather. Our equipment had been soaked during filming on the Spenser Road. Both the tape recorder and the camera had to be repaired as a result. The film was proving to be a very costly venture indeed.

We actually had a lot of fun working on it though. There is a certain humour that seems to come out when city dwellers find themselves operating in a foreign environment. Especially if one of them is me. I mean, I really love gardening and when I was a boy scout, I quite enjoyed camping. But my true place is not in the sodden bush of the West Coast.

On one occasion at least, I sank into deep wet mud up to my thigh on that blessed road we were filming. And really there is not much you can do but laugh. After you've cursed every tree, bird and person in sight that is.

Tim was still pulling the surprises on us each trip too. When we first arrived, for instance, the family owned two horses. One of them was a small black pony that the elder girl, Joella rode. The other was a big brown ex-racehorse called Prince. He was more of an old friend than anything. Sometimes the younger daughter would climb up on his broad back and take him for a walk. That was as much as he could manage. It was painfully obvious that his racing days were distant memories for the beast. Nevertheless, he was very much a part of the scene. Until one trip we made.

We were sitting in the house, warming ourselves round the great fire, getting ready to enjoy dinner with the family. I was discussing with Tim what we might film on the following day, when I noticed smoke billowing down from the chimney and into the room. At first, I thought it must be heavy rain that was causing the smoke to backfire. But it wasn't raining, for once.

No, something else was blocking the passage above the crackling fire. It was Prince. Well part of him. He'd been shot and his carcass was lodged in the upper reaches of the chimney being smoked. Tim assured me that the meat would be tasty when it was done, but I declined to sample it. Then Daniel, his eldest son appeared wearing a waistcoat he'd made from the horse's hide. They certainly were a practical family. Dear Old Prince was serving them even when his useful days were deemed to be over. They assured me that the old chap was literally on his last legs when they decided to release him.

Nothing need be wasted though. It was part of the philosophy. When Tim chopped down trees to clear land he was only fulfilling part of the cycle. The original seed had been nurtured by the heat of the sun. The strength of the tree contained that essence. So it was perfectly justifiable to use the wood to re-create the heat by igniting it. To provide warmth at times when the sun couldn't. The same simple logic convinced Tim to build his windmill. The main supports for the structure had been supplied by a cyclone.

At the back of the house, forming a barrier against the wind, a row of majestic cypresses had stood proudly for seventy years or more. Then in 1972, cyclone Allyson swept through the valley. The same wind that unceremoniously ripped off the roof of the house, toppled three of the tall trees. Ever since they had lain, uprooted, but still living, across the roof of the home-made A-frame.

They were the inspiration for the next project. Tim's reasoning was this. The victims of the force of the wind, would be used in a positive way to harness the wind. Who could argue with that? The windmill would be a great blessing for everyone. Jos would have her wheat ground for her in great quantities instead of having to cajole the children to labour on the little hand grinder. Tim would be able to cut his wood by circular saw instead of the constantly exhausting chopping by axe. And I would have a spectacular finish for my film. If it was constructed in time.

So, now we had the three areas of work going on. The clearing of the land which would become the grazing ground. The building of a road through the dense bush of the Kongahu, and the construction of a giant windmill. Right across the Spenser Road. The public road that had led Tim Vos to Corbyvale in the first place. The symbolism was overwhelming. And so was the effort.

By the time we made our fifth visit, we were all getting a bit tired. But much had been accomplished. The clearing was growing, much of the road was stable and the windmill was complete.

All I needed for my final shots was wind, from the right quarter, to turn the massive sails. We waited all week. The West Coast was as still as a Buddhist garden. We could wait no longer. Already we had gone over budget on the film. This just had to be our last visit to Corbyvale, come what may. So, we had to create our own wind, or achieve the same effect anyway. I just couldn't conceive the documentary finishing without those sails swirling to a grand climax.

Fortunately, right on the day. of our last chance, a friend of Tim's turned up at the house. So I enlisted his help. He and the fearless Hammond Peek entered the interior of the windmill, out of sight of the camera, and turned the sails by hand.

It was beautiful, if you didn't look too closely at the scene. There was Tim, driving his cartload of wood along the reclaimed road towards the windmill. And there was the huge structure standing proud, with its massive sails flailing round at great speed. Whilst in the background, the trees in the bush were motionless. Watching in awe, you might say.

The irony is that a few weeks after we'd finished, when we were editing the thousands upon thousands of feet of film, the winds did come. From the right quarter too but with a vengeance. The windmill was blown down.

In 1978, after the film had been shown on television, the Vos family moved on into the next chapter of their lives. Indeed, their story perhaps had reached its climax. With some other friends who shared their ideals and aspirations they bought five hundred acres of land. Their own land, that they could do what they liked on without fear of being turfed off at short notice.

Interestingly enough, the location of the land is an area quite near to where Tim's dream had first led him. Across the boulders.

About The Author

Hugh Hanafi Hayes was born in London, England and after two years of undistinguished service in the RAF, he developed what is sometimes called an inconsistent work record. In England, Canada, the USA, New Zealand and Australia - where he currently lives - he has been a proofreader, an actor, a radio announcer, a television journalist, an award-winning script writer and a documentary film-maker and producer. He is married to a Canadian born artist and they have six children.

Printed in Great Britain
by Amazon.co.uk, Ltd.,
Marston Gate.